I0825013

SWEET
·SPICY·
STICKY

SWEET SPICY STICKY

OVER 60 CRAVE-WORTHY RECIPES FROM WINGS & RIBS TO DRIZZLES & DIPS

RYLAND PETERS & SMALL

Senior Designer Toni Kay
Senior Editor Abi Waters
Head of Production
Patricia Harrington
Creative Director Leslie Harrington
Editorial Director Julia Charles

Indexer Vanessa Bird

First published in 2026 by
Ryland Peters & Small,
20–21 Jockey's Fields,
London WC1R 4BW
and
1452 Davis Bugg Road,
Warrenton, NC 27589

www.rylandpeters.com
email: euregulations@rylandpeters.com

Note: Some recipes in this book have been previously published by Ryland Peters & Small. See page 144 for full text and photography credits.

ISBN: 978-1-78879-760-3

10 9 8 7 6 5 4 3 2 1

A CIP record for this book is available from the British Library.

US Library of Congress cataloging-in-publication data has been applied for.

The authorised representative in the EEA is
Authorised Rep Compliance Ltd.,
Ground Floor, 71 Lower
Baggot Street, Dublin,
D02 P593, Ireland
www.arccompliance.com

Printed and bound in China.

NOTES

- Both British (Metric) and American (Imperial plus US cup) measurements are included in these recipes for your convenience – however it is important to work with one set of measurements and not alternate between the two within a recipe.
- All spoon measurements are level unless specified.
- All eggs are medium (UK) or large (US), unless specified as large, in which case US extra-large should be used. Uncooked or partially cooked eggs should not be served to the elderly or frail, young children, pregnant women or those with compromised immune systems.
- Ovens should be preheated to the specified temperatures. We recommend using an oven thermometer. If using a fan-assisted oven, adjust temperatures according to the manufacturer's instructions.
- When a recipe calls for the grated zest of citrus fruit, buy unwaxed fruit and wash well before using. If you can only find treated fruit, scrub well in warm soapy water before using.

CONTENTS

INTRODUCTION

Craving hot honey drizzled over everything? Is your mouth watering at the thought of a sticky chicken wing? Is no summer barbecue complete without tender ribs rubbed down with a sweet and smoky spice blend? Then this collection of recipes is for you.

Sweet, sticky and spicy is a distinct flavour profile that ticks all the boxes when it comes to deeply satisfying food. Pair spicy heat with sticky sweetness and often a little warming smokiness too by cleverly combining everyday ingredients such as honey and habanero, maple and chipotle and pineapple and chilli to create culinary alchemy.

This cookbook is all about balancing the rich sweetness that makes your taste buds dance, the fiery kick that awakens the senses and that irresistible sticky goodness that clings to your fingers and keeps you coming back for more.

Whether you're a fan of sizzling, spicy wings, rich and sticky ribs or savoury dishes with unbeatable taste, you'll find something in these pages to satisfy your cravings. This collection celebrates the art of combining contrasting flavours into dishes that are bold, comforting and unforgettable.

Find every recipe you need here, from glazed chicken wings, BBQ sauce-drenched ribs and melt-in-the-mouth spice-rubbed pulled pork, to sweet potato wedges served with Sriracha mayonnaise for dipping or a simple cheese plate drizzled with irresistibly spicy hot honey.

These creative ideas for everyday snacks, meals and food to impress your friends are guaranteed to tantalize those taste buds every time.

So, roll up your sleeves, embrace the messiness of it all and get ready to dive into a world where sweet meets spicy and everything gets sticky. Let's turn up the heat and get cooking!

SMALL BITES

This traditional dish has found its way onto most modern Japanese restaurant menus – that's how good it is. The sweet and savoury umami notes coupled with the melty texture of the grilled aubergine/eggplant make it sublimely satisfying. The best way to enjoy this dish is to scoop out the miso-caramelly flesh with a spoon. Eaten with a bowl of rice, it also makes a great meal for one.

MISO-GLAZED AUBERGINE

2 aubergines/eggplants
4 tbsp toasted sesame oil
4 tbsp vegetable oil
1 tbsp crushed roasted hazelnuts, to serve

MISO GLAZE

5 tbsp brown rice miso
2 tbsp soft light brown sugar
1 tbsp mirin
1 tbsp sake

MAKES 8

Peel strips of skin off the aubergines lengthways (alternately leaving a strip, then peeling a strip) to create a striped pattern. Top and tail each aubergine, then slice each one widthways into 3-cm/1¼-inch thick round slices.

Use a sharp knife to score a cross-hatch pattern onto each side of the aubergine slices. This technique is called a 'hidden cut', and it helps the vegetables to cook quickly and lets flavours penetrate.

Preheat the grill/broiler to 180°C/350°F or to the medium setting.

Place the aubergine slices on a baking sheet and drizzle with the toasted sesame oil and vegetable oil. Grill/broil the vegetables for 15 minutes until lightly browned and tender.

In the meantime, make the miso glaze. Combine the brown rice miso, brown sugar, mirin and sake with 1½ tablespoons water in a small saucepan. Simmer over a low heat for about 1 minute, stirring with a spatula, until the mixture is combined and glossy. Set aside.

When the aubergine slices are lightly browned and tender, remove them from the grill and spread the miso glaze on top. Return to the grill for 4–5 minutes, or until bubbling.

Sprinkle the aubergine slices with crushed hazelnuts to serve.

This is a Chinese-inspired fusion-style dish with healthy tofu at its core and fresh plums used to make a sweet, spicy and sticky dipping sauce. There are quite a lot of processes involved to give the tofu the perfect texture, but you can save time by using a ready-made plum sauce, if you like.

SWEET & SOUR POPCORN TOFU

6 tbsp light soy sauce
2 tsp Chinese five-spice powder
400 g/14 oz. firm tofu, drained, excess water pressed out and sliced into small cubes
150 g/1 cup cornflour/cornstarch
100 ml/1/3 cup soya/soy cream
150 g/2 3/4 cups panko breadcrumbs
1 tsp hot smoked paprika
600 ml/2 1/2 cups vegetable oil, for deep-frying

PLUM SAUCE

12 plums, stoned/pitted and roughly chopped
4–6 tbsp soft brown sugar
8 tbsp rice vinegar, or to taste
1 tbsp tomato purée/paste
1/2 tsp salt

SERVES 4–6

To make the sauce, put the plums in a pan over a medium heat and add the sugar and 2 tablespoons water. Bring to the boil, then simmer for 15 minutes, or until the fruit is completely softened. Add the remaining sauce ingredients and bring to a simmer again, adding a little more water if necessary so that the sauce is not too thick. Using a food processor or blender, blend the sauce until smooth. Check the seasoning and adjust the sugar, salt or vinegar to taste. The balance of sweet and sour flavours means one should not overpower the other.

Mix the soy sauce and five-spice powder in a bowl, then drizzle this marinade over the tofu pieces. Put the cornflour in one bowl, the soya cream in another bowl and the panko breadcrumbs in a separate third bowl. Add the paprika to the breadcrumbs and mix well.

Heat the vegetable oil in a wok over a medium–high heat.

Put a sheet of non-stick baking parchment on the work surface. Dip each piece of tofu in the cornflour, then in the soya cream and then in the breadcrumbs, shaping it a little to form a ball. Lay each coated ball on the baking parchment as you go.

Fry the tofu in the hot oil in batches until golden brown and crispy. Lift out using a slotted spoon and drain on paper towels. You can keep the tofu balls warm in a low oven, if you like, or reheat them later at 180°C/160°C fan/350°F/gas 4 for 10–15 minutes. Serve with the plum sauce.

If you want to surprise and delight guests at a party, this dish is for you. These unusual little boats are actually nori chips holding spicy tuna tartare!

SPICY TUNA TARTARE ON NORI CHIPS

300 g/10½ oz. sashimi-grade tuna loin

½ pear, peeled, cored and diced into small pieces

NORI CHIPS

3 nori sheets, each sheet cut into 8 triangles

750 ml/3¼ cups vegetable oil, for frying

2 tbsp potato starch

CHILLI SAUCE

1½ tbsp gochujang chilli paste

1 tbsp soy sauce

2 tsp sake

pinch of light brown soft sugar

¼ tsp grated garlic

½ tbsp toasted sesame oil

1 tbsp mayonnaise

TO SERVE

10 g/⅓ oz. fresh chives, roughly chopped

1 tbsp toasted sesame seeds

MAKES 24

To make a light batter for the chips, mix the potato starch with 100 ml/⅓ cup cold water in a mixing bowl and stir. Set aside.

Put the vegetable oil in a heavy-based, wide frying pan/skillet or wok over a high heat and bring the temperature to 180°C/350°F. To test that the oil is hot enough, dip a nori chip in the batter and gently drop it into the hot oil. If it sizzles gently with bubbles around the chip, it is the right temperature. Reduce the heat to medium to maintain the oil temperature while you fry all the chips.

One at a time, dip the nori triangles into the batter to evenly coat all over, then quickly but carefully drop into the hot oil from front to back (or away from you) to ensure you don't splash any oil on yourself. The nori chip will start sizzling quickly, as it contains water, but will dry within 10 seconds and be ready for turning. Turn it over to cook the other side for 20 seconds or until the bubbles disappear and the batter turns crispy. Remove the nori chip from the hot oil with a slotted spoon and leave to drain on a cooling rack. Repeat for the remaining nori triangles and batter. These cook quickly so you can cook one at a time or up to 4–5 in one go, just don't overcrowd the pan. The batter may separate if left out for a while, so just stir well before you dip the nori.

To make the tuna tartare, finely chop the tuna to a minced texture with a sharp knife, discarding any hard white sinew. Place the minced tuna and pear in a glass or metal bowl. Mix the chilli sauce ingredients together in a separate bowl, then pour the chilli sauce over the tuna and mix until well combined. Cover and keep the tartare in the fridge for at least 20 minutes and up to half a day until you are ready to serve. (Leaving it a little while helps the flavours to develop.)

Spread the spicy tuna tartare on the nori chips. Sprinkle with chopped chives and toasted sesame seeds and serve immediately.

The soft flesh of the salmon works wonderfully with this sweet and sticky marinade and the hints of orange really add fragrance to this hassle-free recipe.

MISO & MAPLE MARINATED SALMON

500 g/1 lb. 2 oz. skin-on salmon fillet, scaled and pin-boned
1/2 tsp fine sea salt
1 tbsp toasted white sesame seeds, to garnish
a bunch of fresh chives

MISO & MAPLE MARINADE
90 g/3 oz. sweet white miso (saikyo miso)
2 tbsp mirin
2 tbsp maple syrup
2 tsp finely grated orange zest, plus extra for garnishing
1 tsp peeled and finely grated fresh ginger

PICKLED CAULIFLOWER
1 cauliflower
120 ml/1/2 cup rice vinegar
4 tbsp caster/granulated sugar
2 tsp salt
1 dried chilli (optional)

baking sheet lined with baking parchment
bamboo skewers

MAKES 20 BITES

Dice the salmon into 3-cm/1¼-inch square cubes, then sprinkle it with the salt and set aside for 20 minutes. Wipe off any excess moisture from the fish with paper towels.

To make the miso and maple marinade, combine the sweet white miso, mirin, maple syrup, orange zest and ginger in a bowl. Place the diced salmon in a container with a lid, pour over the marinade and gently stir together. Seal the container and leave to marinate for at least 30 minutes or up to 24 hours in the fridge.

To pickle the cauliflower, bring a medium saucepan of water to the boil. Meanwhile, cut the cauliflower into 20 equal, bite-sized florets. Add the cauliflower to the pan and boil for 2 minutes. Drain well, then put the cauliflower into a container with an airtight lid or in a resealable bag.

Mix the rice vinegar, sugar, salt and chilli (if using) together with 120 ml/1/2 cup water in a jug/pitcher, then pour the pickling liquid over the top of the cauliflower. If you are using a container, shake the container to make sure each piece of cauliflower is coated in pickling liquid. Or, if you are using a resealable bag, dip the bag in a bowl of cold water to remove any air and seal immediately so it is almost vacuum-packed. Leave to marinate for at least 30 minutes or up to 24 hours in the fridge.

When you are nearly ready to serve, preheat the oven to 220°C/200°C fan/425°F/gas 7.

Gently wipe most of the marinade off the salmon with a butter knife or palette knife. Place the salmon, skin-side up, on the lined baking sheet and bake in the preheated oven for 7 minutes (depending on the thickness of salmon) until cooked and slightly browned.

To serve, skewer a piece of cauliflower, then a piece of salmon from the skin side. Sprinkle over some orange zest and sesame seeds to garnish. Place the skewers on a bed of fresh chives to serve.

You could roast and serve a whole duck if you want it crispy, but it will take a couple of hours. This recipe uses just duck breast to save time on roasting and shredding – it's juicy and easy to portion. The sticky plums add a little heat and look gorgeous too.

CHINESE DUCK BREAST PANCAKES WITH GINGER JAMMY PLUMS

175 g/6 oz. duck breast

2 tsp Chinese five spice mixed with 1/2 teaspoon salt

10 ready-made Chinese pancakes (about 14 cm/ 5 1/2 inches in diameter)

10 tsp hoisin sauce

1/2 cucumber, cut into matchsticks

5 spring onions/scallions, cut into matchsticks

GINGER JAMMY PLUMS

2 fresh plums, stoned/pitted and cut into 20 wedges

freshly squeezed juice of 1 orange

1 tsp grated fresh ginger

1 tsp caster/granulated sugar

MAKES 20

To make the jammy plums, simmer the plums in the orange juice, ginger and sugar for 3 minutes in a shallow frying pan/ skillet until they take on a jam-like texture.

Take the duck out of the fridge 20 minutes before cooking. Score the skin of the duck and trim off any excess fat around the sides. Rub the five spice and salt mix all over the duck. Put it in a frying pan/skillet skin-side down and turn on the heat.

When the pan is hot and you can hear the duck start to sizzle, let it cook for 5 minutes.

Sear the duck on the sides and the bottom, cooking for a further 5–8 minutes, or until cooked to your liking. Take the pan off the heat and leave the duck to rest.

Lay the pancakes flat on a chopping board and cut in half. Spoon 1/2 teaspoon hoisin sauce on a half-pancake and arrange a piece of duck, a plum wedge and some cucumber and spring onions/scallions on top. Tightly roll into a flat cone. Repeat with the remaining ingredients before serving.

These popular Japanese pancakes are topped with a rich and sticky okonomiyaki sauce and your choice of toppings for a personal touch.

SAVOURY PANCAKES WITH TOPPINGS

PANCAKE MIX

250 g/1¾ cups plus 2 tbsp plain/all-purpose flour

2 tsp baking powder

300 ml/1¼ cups chilled dashi stock

4 UK large/US extra-large eggs

500 g/1 lb. 2 oz. green or white cabbage, finely chopped

4 spring onions/scallions, finely chopped

150 g/1 cup canned sweetcorn

20 g/¾ oz. yamaimo (Japanese mountain yam), peeled and finely grated (simply omit if you cannot find it)

vegetable oil, for frying

OPTIONAL TOPPINGS

4 very thin slices of pork belly

4 raw prawns/shrimp, peeled and deveined

1 fresh squid, cut into rings

100 g/1 packed cup plus 2 tbsp grated Cheddar cheese

TO SERVE

240 g/1 cup okonomiyaki sauce

180 g/¾ cup Japanese mayonnaise

20 g/¾ oz. bonito flakes

4 tsp nori seaweed flakes (optional)

MAKES 12

To make the pancake mix, sift the flour and baking powder into a bowl and then pour in the chilled dashi slowly, stirring to incorporate and break up any lumps of flour. Don't overmix or the mixture will become tough. Refrigerate for 15 minutes.

Meanwhile, place the eggs in a separate large bowl and stir in the cabbage. Beat vigorously with a wooden spoon to create lots of fine bubbles and an airy texture. Gently add the spring onions and sweetcorn and stir in until evenly combined.

Remove the pancake mix from the fridge and mix in the yam. Add the pancake mix to the cabbage mixture in three batches, stirring gently with every addition until combined.

Heat a large frying pan/skillet over a high heat. When hot, add enough oil to lightly coat the surface of the pan. Using a large serving spoon, spoon three batches of pancake mixture into the pan. Reduce the heat to medium, then scatter over your favourite toppings on the surface of the three pancakes while still wet. Cook for 2 minutes until small bubbles appear around the edges of the pancakes and the underneaths have turned brown. Don't press down on the panackes as they cook or they will become hard. Carefully turn the pancakes over and cook for a further 4–6 minutes, depending on thickness and what toppings you have used. Peek underneath to check whether the toppings are nicely cooked, then turn the pancake over again if you are happy and cook for 1 more minute on the first side. Repeat with the remaining mixture and toppings and serve immediately on individual plates.

For a nice decoration, spread okonomiyaki sauce all over the pancakes with the back of a spoon, then squeeze the Japanese mayonnaise over in parallel horizontal lines. Drag a toothpick through across the mayonnaise at intervals to create an attractive pattern. Sprinkle with bonito and seaweed flakes and for extra seasoning, if desired.

Here, slow-cooked juicy confit duck is spiced with five-spice, star anise, cinnamon and cloves, and enclosed in puff pastry to make these delectable treats with a delicious sweet and sticky filling.

HOISIN DUCK PUFFS

2 duck legs
60 g/¼ cup sea salt flakes, plus extra for serving
1 tbsp freshly ground black pepper
1 garlic clove, crushed
2 tbsp Chinese five-spice powder
5 star anise
1 cinnamon stick
2 cloves
500 g/1 lb. duck fat
2 spring onions/scallions, chopped
2 tbsp hoisin sauce
1 packet of ready-rolled puff pastry
1 egg, beaten
white sesame seeds, to garnish

small round pastry cutter
2 large baking sheets, greased

MAKES 12

Rub the duck legs with the sea salt flakes, black pepper, crushed garlic clove, five-spice powder, star anise, cinnamon stick and cloves. Pack the duck and these ingredients tightly into a dish, skin-side down. Cover the dish with cling film/plastic wrap and leave to marinate in the fridge for 24 hours.

Preheat the oven to 150°C/130°C fan/300°F/gas 2.

Scrape the marinade off the duck pieces. Heat the duck fat in an ovenproof dish until melted, then add the duck legs, ensuring they are completely submerged.

Bake the duck in the preheated oven for 3½ hours, or until the meat is very tender when pierced with a skewer and the fat in the skin is rendered. Once cooked, remove the duck from the fat and leave to cool uncovered. Shred finely and mix with the chopped spring onions and hoisin sauce.

Using a small round pastry cutter, stamp out 24 rounds from the puff pastry. Put a spoonful of filling on one round, brush the edges with beaten egg and position a second round of pastry on top. Use a fork to make indentations around the edge to tightly seal. Repeat with the remaining pastry rounds and duck filling to make 12 puffs.

Preheat the oven to 200°C/180°C fan/400°F/gas 6.

Brush the tops with beaten egg and sprinkle with white sesame seeds. Place on the prepared baking sheets and bake in the preheated oven for 20–25 minutes until golden brown.

Light flaky pastry is here the yin to the yang of the dark and richly sticky barbecue pork to make these irresistible barbecue pork puffs. They make a great party canape or light bite for sharing with friends.

BARBECUE PORK PUFFS

1 tbsp sunflower oil
1 shallot, chopped
2 tbsp dry sherry
225 g/8 oz. pork loin, diced
1 tsp crushed garlic
2 tbsp honey
2 tbsp hoisin sauce
1 tsp Chinese five-spice powder
1 tbsp soy sauce
1 packet of ready-rolled puff pastry
1 egg, beaten
black sesame seeds, to garnish

heat-proof casserole dish
2 large baking sheets, greased

MAKES 12

For the filling, heat the oil in the heatproof casserole dish and add the chopped shallot. Cook for 5–7 minutes until softened and lightly caramelized. Pour in the sherry and let the alcohol cook out. Lower the heat to medium and add the diced pork. Cook, stirring, for a further 2 minutes or until lightly browned.

Meanwhile, mix the garlic, honey, hoisin sauce, five-spice powder and soy sauce in a bowl with 2 tablespoons of water. Add this to the pork and shallot, stirring well. Cover and cook for 1 hour over a low heat until the sauce has thickened and the pork is soft. Check occasionally during cooking to ensure the sauce does not dry out, adding a little extra water if needed.

Preheat the oven to 200°C/180°C fan/400°F/gas 6. Finely chop the pork once it is cool, ready for filling the pastry.

Cut the pastry into 24 small squares by cutting the sheet into 6 strips widthways and then each strip into 4 squares. Put a small tablespoon of filling on one pastry square, brush the edges with beaten egg and position a second piece of pastry on top. Use a fork to make indentations and to tightly seal the edges. Repeat with the remaining pastry squares and filling to make 12 barbecue pork puffs.

Place the parcels on the greased baking sheets, brush the tops with beaten egg and sprinkle with black sesame seeds. Bake in the preheated oven for 20–25 minutes or until golden brown.

SNACKS & STREET FOOD

Barbecue Pork Bao

Hirata Steamed Pork Buns

Grilled Chicken Skewers

Beef Bulgogi & Rice Noodle Wraps

Burmese-style Spiced Pork with Sweet Garlic Sauce

Duck Satay with Grilled Pineapple & Plum Sauce

Charred Shrimp with Nam Jim

Teriyaki Burger

Teriyaki Sauce

Kalua Chipotle Ketchup

Chipotle Crema

Crispy Shallots

Kimchi & Meatball Pizza with Soy–lime Glaze

Maple-cured Bacon & Tomato Sandwich

The pillowy-soft bread bun surrounding char siu-style pork is a heavenly combo.

BARBECUE PORK BAO

1 batch bread dough (see below)
1 tbsp sunflower oil
1 shallot, chopped
2 tbsp dry sherry
350 g/12 oz. pork loin, diced
1 tsp crushed/minced garlic
2 tbsp runny honey
2 tbsp hoisin sauce
1 tsp Chinese five-spice powder
1 tbsp soy sauce

BREAD DOUGH

2 tsp dry easy-bake yeast
450 g/3½ cups Asian white wheat flour
100 g/¾ cup plus 1 tbsp icing sugar/confectioners' sugar, sifted
15 g/2 tbsp dried milk powder
¼ tsp salt
2 tsp baking powder
50 ml/scant ¼ cup vegetable oil, plus extra for oiling the bowl

a bamboo steamer, lined with parchment paper

MAKES 16

Place the yeast in a large mixing bowl, then add the flour, sugar, milk powder, salt and baking powder. Make sure the yeast is separated from the salt by the layer of flour. Add the water and oil and bring together with a dough scraper. When no dry flour remains, remove the dough from the bowl and place on a lightly floured surface. Knead firmly for 10 minutes, or until smooth and elastic. Lightly oil the mixing bowl. Shape the dough into two cylinders and place back in the oiled bowl. Cover with oiled cling film/plastic wrap and leave in a warm place to rise for 40–60 minutes or until doubled in size.

To make the filling, heat the oil in a heatproof casserole dish and add the shallot. Cook over a medium heat for about 5–7 minutes. Pour in the sherry and let the alcohol cook out for a few minutes. Lower the heat a little and add the pork. Cook, stirring, for a further 2 minutes or until lightly browned.

Meanwhile, in a separate bowl mix the garlic, honey, hoisin sauce, Chinese five-spice powder and soy sauce with 2 tablespoons water. Add this to the pork and shallot mixture. Stir well. Cover and cook over a low heat for 1 hour or until the sauce has thickened and the pork is tender. Add a little extra water if necessary.

Remove the risen dough from the bowl, punch it down and knead it again briefly. Roll the dough out into a big rectangle and portion it out into 16 equal balls. Cover the dough balls with oiled cling film and leave to rest again for 30 minutes in a warm place.

Roll out each dough ball so that it has a diameter of about 7.5 cm/ 3 inches. Place a heaped tablespoon of filling in the centre of each round. Gather the edges to form pleats and pinch to seal the top of the bun. Set the buns into a lined bamboo steamer at least 5 cm/2 inches apart. Cover with oiled cling film and allow to rise for 30 minutes. Steam the buns over boiling water for 8–10 minutes until the dough is fluffy. Let cool slightly and serve.

This recipe for sticky caramelized pork belly inside soft bao buns is absolutely mouth-watering. It can be prepared in stages, if liked, and you can customize the filling by adding some pickled carrot or shavings of spring onion/scallion. Or mix up the filling all together and use slow-cooked beef or chicken instead.

HIRATA STEAMED PORK BUNS

HIRATA PORK BELLY

400-g/14-oz. piece pork belly
3½ tbsp each sake, mirin and soy sauce
4 tsp white sugar
500 ml/2 cups chicken stock
5 sancho peppercorns
1 star anise
1 whole dried chilli/chile
salt and pepper, to season
olive oil, for frying

STEAMED BUNS

1 tsp dry active yeast
200 ml/1 cup warm water
450 g/scant 3½ cups plain/all-purpose flour, plus extra for dusting
60 g/scant ⅓ cup caster/granulated sugar
¾ tsp baking powder
50 g/¼ cup double/heavy cream
sunflower oil, for brushing

BBQ KETCHUP

3 tbsp vegetable oil
2 tsp crushed garlic
2 tsp grated ginger
125 ml/½ cup Shaoxing rice wine
3 tbsp gochujang paste
70 g/⅓ cup white sugar
16–17 cherry tomatoes
3½ tbsp oyster sauce
2½ tbsp soy sauce
3½ tbsp tamarind water
200 ml/¾–1 cup pork cooking liquid
freshly squeezed lime juice

DRESSED CUCUMBER

½ cucumber
100 ml/⅓ cup mirin
1 tbsp white sugar
coriander/cilantro, to serve

stand mixer with a dough hook
10 squares of 10 x 10 cm/ 4 x 4 inch non-stick baking parchment, greased
bamboo or metal steamer
cook's blowtorch (optional)

MAKES 10 BUNS

To make the hirata pork belly, season the meat with salt and pepper and remove the rind. Preheat a little oil in a large, deep pan and sear the pork over a high heat to caramelize the fat. Remove the meat from the pan and set aside. Add the sake to the hot pan and flame very carefully using a match. When the alcohol has burnt off, add the mirin, soy sauce and sugar and stir. Return the meat to the pan and cover with chicken stock. Add the peppercorns, star anise and chilli. Cover and simmer gently for 3 hours (or cook in the oven at 140°C/120°C fan/280°F/gas 1) until the meat is falling apart.

Remove the pork and sieve/strain the contents of the pan. Discard the aromatics and keep the liquid to use in the BBQ ketchup. Leave the pork to cool and then keep in the fridge until required.

To make the steamed buns, dissolve the yeast in the warm water and leave until frothy. Put all the other dough ingredients (apart from the oil) into the bowl of a stand mixer with the dough hook. Add the yeast water and knead with the dough hook for 5 minutes until combined into a smooth dough. Transfer to a clean bowl and cover with cling film/plastic wrap. Rest in a warm place for 1 hour or until doubled in size.

Divide the risen dough into ten equal parts and roll each portion out on a lightly floured surface into small

PYREX

ovals, about the thickness and shape of a pitta bread. Fold each of these in half widthways and place onto the prepared squares of baking parchment on a baking sheet. Add a small piece of greased baking parchment to the fold of each bun to stop them sticking together at the fold. Brush the buns with the oil, cover the tray loosely with cling film and leave in a warm place to rise for 15 minutes.

Preheat the water for the steamer. Use the parchment to transfer the buns to the steamer and cook for about 12 minutes. The steamer should not be overcrowded so you may need to do this in a few batches.

To make the BBQ ketchup, heat the oil in a frying pan/skillet and fry the garlic and ginger until fragrant. Deglaze the pan with the Shaoxing rice wine, then stir in the gochujang paste and sugar. Cook for a few minutes until caramelized, then mix in all the remaining ingredients (apart from the lime juice). Cook for 5–10 minutes until reduced and the tomatoes have softened. Remove from the heat and pass through a sieve/strainer. Add a squeeze of lime juice to season and set aside to cool.

To make the cucumber, deseed and shred the cucumber. Boil the mirin and sugar with 3 tablespoons water. Mix with the cucumber and set aside.

To construct the buns, slice the pork belly into 2 cm/¾ inch thick slices. Heat a frying pan with a little oil and fry the pork slices over a medium-high heat for 2 minutes on each side. Deglaze the pan with a little of the ketchup and turn off the heat. To give the buns a nice crisp finish use a cook's blowtorch to quickly sear the dough. Place a slice of pork in each bun with a little of the cucumber and some of the BBQ ketchup. Garnish with fresh coriander and serve.

The sweet and sticky basting sauce makes these chicken skewers absolutely delicious.

GRILLED CHICKEN SKEWERS

Soak the cabbage in a bowl of cold water for 10 minutes, then drain well and keep in the fridge until you are ready to serve it.

To make the yakitori sauce, combine the ingredients in a small saucepan. Simmer over a medium-low heat for about 8 minutes, stirring occasionally, until slightly thickened. Set aside.

Thread each soaked wooden skewer with a piece of spring onion, followed by a piece of chicken with the skin side facing outwards. Repeat the same process once more for each skewer, and finish each skewer with a slice of mushroom. Turn the skin of the chicken to the same side on each skewer so you can cook the skin side first to draw the fat out of it.

To fry the yakitori, heat a large frying pan/skillet over a high heat. Add ½ tablespoon oil, then put six of the skewers, skin side-down, into the pan. Turn the heat down to medium and fry for 5 minutes. Carefully remove most of the fat from the pan, then turn the skewers over and cook the other side for 3 more minutes.

Pour half of the yakitori sauce over the chicken skewers, then simmer for about 2 minutes until caramelized. Turn the skewers in the sauce to make sure all the ingredients are coated. Remove the skewers to a plate and repeat the cooking process with the remaining skewers and yakitori sauce.

Heat any remaining sauce in a small saucepan and simmer for 5 minutes until thickened and hot to serve alongside the chicken.

Combine all the ingredients for the tosazu sauce in a small bowl or jar. Place the cabbage on a large serving plate, then pour the tosazu all over the cabbage. Serve alongside the hot chicken skewers with shichimi spice mix and/or yuzu kosho.

NOTE *Alternatively, you can grill/broil the skewers if you prefer: preheat the grill/broiler to 200°C/400°F or to medium-high. Place the skewers on a grill/broiler pan with a rim and grill for 10 minutes. Brush the yakitori sauce over the chicken, then grill for another 10 minutes, brushing them with more sauce and turning them a couple more times as they cook.*

1 sweetheart (pointy) cabbage, root and outer leaves removed, torn into bite-sized pieces

4 spring onions/scallions or baby leeks, cut into 3-cm/1¼-inch lengths

650 g/1 lb. 7 oz. skin-on boneless chicken thighs, diced into bite-sized pieces (you should get 4–6 pieces from one thigh)

6 fresh shiitake mushrooms, stems removed and halved

1 tbsp vegetable oil, for frying

shichimi spice mix and/or yuzu kosho, to serve

YAKITORI SAUCE

60 ml/¼ cup soy sauce

30 ml/2 tbsp mirin

30 ml/2 tbsp sake

1 tbsp light brown soft sugar

TOSAZU SAUCE

90 ml/⅓ cup dashi

3 tbsp rice vinegar

3 tbsp mirin

3 tbsp light soy sauce

12 wooden skewers (roughly 15 cm/6 inches long), soaked in cold water for 15 minutes

MAKES 12 SKEWERS

The word bulgogi means 'fire meat' and refers to marinated and grilled meats, usually beef. Here it is stir-fried and combined with shiitake mushrooms and Korean sweet potato noodles, wrapped in lettuce leaves and topped with kimchi and ssamjang.

BEEF BULGOGI & RICE NOODLE WRAPS

Begin by preparing the beef. Thinly slice the steak and arrange in a single layer in a wide, shallow dish. Combine the soy sauce, sugar, shallot, garlic, sesame oil and Chinese five-spice powder, and pour over the beef. Set aside to marinate for at least 1 hour.

Plunge the sweet potato noodles into a pan of boiling water and cook for 4–5 minutes until al dente. Drain, refresh under cold water and drain again. Shake the noodles dry and dress with a little sesame oil to prevent them from sticking together. Set aside.

Heat the oil in a wok or large frying pan/skillet set over a medium heat until it starts to shimmer. Add the beef in batches and stir-fry for 2–3 minutes until golden. Remove with a slotted spoon. Add the mushrooms and any remaining marinade and stir-fry for 1 minute. Return the beef to the pan along with the noodles and stir-fry for 1 minute until everything is heated through.

Serve with lettuce leaves, kimchi and the ssamjang Korean spicy sauce. Wrap, roll and eat.

500 g/1 lb. beef rib-eye steak
2 tbsp light or dark soy sauce
2 tbsp soft brown sugar
1 Asian shallot, finely chopped
1 garlic clove, crushed
2 tsp sesame oil, plus extra for dressing
½ tsp Chinese five-spice powder
125 g/4 oz. spiralized sweet potato noodles
2 tbsp peanut oil
125 g/4 oz. shiitake mushrooms, trimmed and cut into quarters

TO SERVE
lettuce leaves
4 tbsp kimchi
ssamjang (Korean spicy sauce)

SERVES 4

This recipe is typical of the type of dishes regularly cooked by street-food vendors in Myanmar. Serve with rice and lots of lovely fresh Asian herbs – basil, coriander/cilantro and mint – and a good squeeze of lime juice.

BURMESE-STYLE SPICED PORK WITH SWEET GARLIC SAUCE

500 g/1 lb. 2 oz. pork fillet, very thinly sliced
2 tsp ground turmeric
¼ tsp salt
3 tbsp fish sauce
sunflower oil, for deep-frying
boiled rice, fresh herbs and lime wedges, to serve

TAMARIND SAUCE

2 large garlic cloves
4 red chillies/chiles, chopped
1 tbsp peanut or sunflower oil
4 tbsp tamarind paste
4 tbsp grated palm sugar
2–3 tbsp soy sauce

8 metal skewers

SERVES 4

Place the sliced pork in a bowl and add the turmeric and salt. Rub gently to lightly coat the meat, then stir in the fish sauce. Cover and refrigerate for at least 4 hours.

Remove from the fridge 30 minutes before cooking to return to room temperature. Divide the meat between 8 skewers, threading a few slices onto each one, arrange on a large platter and set aside until required.

To make the sauce, place the garlic and chillies in a pestle and mortar or a blender and pound or blend until you have a rough paste. Heat the oil in a small frying pan/skillet and gently fry the chilli paste for 2–3 minutes soft and fragrant. Add the tamarind paste, sugar, soy sauce and 50 ml/¼ cup water and simmer for 5 minutes until the sauce is thick and glossy. Keep warm.

Place the pork, tamarind sauce, fresh herbs, lime wedges and some plain boiled rice in bowls on the table.

Pour enough oil into a metal fondue pan to come no more than a third of the way up the sides and heat on the stovetop until it reaches 180°C/350°F. As soon as the oil reaches its required temperature, very carefully transfer the pot to the tabletop burner. Diners can gently lower the pork skewers into the hot oil and cook for 1–2 minutes until crisp, golden and cooked through. Serve with all the accompaniments.

Chicken satays are popular throughout Southeast Asia but in Vietnam, Cambodia and China, duck satays are common too. Duck is often served in the Chinese tradition of sweet and sour with a fruity sauce. You can buy ready-made bottled plum sauce in Chinese markets and most stores.

DUCK SATAY WITH GRILLED PINEAPPLE & PLUM SAUCE

700 g/1 lb. 9 oz. duck breasts or boned thighs, sliced into thin, bite-sized strips

1–2 tbsp groundnut/peanut or coconut oil, for brushing

1 small pineapple, peeled, cored and sliced

Chinese plum sauce, to serve

MARINADE

2–3 tbsp light soy sauce

freshly squeezed juice of 1 lime

1–2 tsp caster/granulated sugar

1–2 garlic cloves, minced

25 g/1 oz. fresh ginger, peeled and grated

1 small onion, grated

1–2 tsp ground coriander/ cilantro

1 tsp salt

a packet of wooden or bamboo skewers, soaked in water before use

SERVES 4

To make the marinade, put the soy sauce and lime juice in a bowl with the sugar and mix until it dissolves. Add the garlic, ginger and grated onion and stir in the coriander and salt.

Place the strips of duck in a bowl and pour over the marinade. Toss well, cover and chill in the refrigerator for at least 4 hours.

Thread the duck strips onto the skewers and brush them with oil. Prepare a charcoal or conventional grill/broiler.

Cook the duck satay for 3–4 minutes on each side until the duck is nicely browned.

Grill the slices of pineapple at the same time. When browned, cut them into bite-sized pieces and serve with the duck.

Drizzle the satay with plum sauce to serve.

This is such a simple yet effective dish and is great for diving into and getting your hands dirty with a big group of friends. The Nam Jim is a wonderfully vibrant Thai sauce that makes these totally addictive. Make sure you use the roots of the coriander/cilantro and not the leaves, as this is where all the flavour is.

CHARRED SHRIMP WITH NAM JIM

8 raw king prawns/jumbo shrimp, shell on

NAM JIM

roots of 1 bunch of fresh coriander/cilantro plus reserved leaves for garnish

2 garlic cloves

2.5-cm/1-inch piece fresh ginger

1 large red chilli/chile, deseeded, plus extra slices for garnish

1 tbsp coconut palm sugar

2 tsp fish sauce

freshly squeezed juice of 1 lime

sea salt

ridged stovetop griddle pan/grill pan

SERVES 3–4

Using a pestle and mortar, pound the coriander roots, garlic, ginger and chilli until you get a paste. This will take a few minutes of fairly aggressive pounding! The skin of the chilli will also come loose so when that happens, you should pick it out and discard it.

Add the sugar and pound, then add a little salt, the fish sauce and lime juice. Mix together and taste. Adjust it ever so slightly until you get the right balance.

Heat a stovetop griddle pan/grill pan over a high heat. Cut the prawns lengthways down the middle of the belly, so you have long halves. Place them, flesh-side down, on the dry pan, cook for 2 minutes, then flip them over and cook for another 2 minutes.

Once cooked, arrange the prawns together on a plate scattered with the reserved coriander leaves and extra chilli slices. Drizzle with Nam Jim and serve.

Affectionately known as 'teri burgers', these are Hawai'i's take on an American classic. The teri sauce gives these burgers a sweet, sticky quality and helps to keep the meat moist and extra succulent. Although frying is suggested here, they are arguably even better cooked on the barbecue or grilled/broiled.

TERIYAKI BURGER

Place the steak in a large bowl with the spring onions, ginger, garlic, pepper, salt, Teriyaki Sauce, panko breadcrumbs and sesame seeds. Mix together well. Divide the mixture into four burgers and shape into round patties, about 2.5 cm/ 1 inch thick.

Heat the oil in a heavy-based frying pan/skillet over a medium-high heat. Fry the burgers for about 4 minutes on each side, or for a little longer if you prefer your burger well-done.

Serve each burger in a warm bun with thinly sliced red onion, lettuce and tomato. Serve with Kahlua Chipotle Ketchup on the side along with your choice of pickles.

NOTE *For an extra tropical twist, try topping each of your burgers with a grilled/broiled pineapple ring.*

450 g/1 lb. minced/ground steak
1 bunch spring onions/ scallions, finely sliced (white and green parts)
1 tsp finely chopped fresh ginger
1 tsp finely chopped garlic
¼ tsp freshly ground black pepper
¼ tsp sea salt
2½ tbsp Teriyaki Sauce (see page 46)
10 g/¼ cup panko breadcrumbs
1 tbsp toasted sesame seeds
2 tbsp vegetable oil

TO SERVE

4 burger buns, warmed (brioche buns work well)
thinly sliced red onion, lettuce and tomato
Kahlua Chipotle Ketchup (see page 46)
your choice of pickles

MAKES 4

This sauce should have a syrupy consistency and a comfortingly sweet but savoury taste. It is frequently used in chicken, salmon and beef dishes, but can dress up noodles, rice or vegetables or be used as a dipping sauce. The cornflour/ cornstarch is just used to thicken the consistency of the sauce, so omit if you want to use it as a marinade.

TERIYAKI SAUCE

120 ml/½ cup soy sauce
1½ tbsp honey
1½ tsp minced fresh ginger
1 tsp minced fresh garlic
2 tbsp mirin
4 tbsp demerara/ turbinado sugar
2 tbsp cornflour/ cornstarch

MAKES ABOUT 350 ML/ SCANT 1½ CUPS

Combine all ingredients, except the cornflour, in a pan. Add 60 ml/¼ cup water and warm gently; do not boil.

Mix the cornflour with 3 tablespoons cold water to make a liquid paste. Whisk this into the sauce until dissolved. Heat gently, stirring frequently, until the sauce begins to thicken to a syrupy consistency, then remove from the heat (the sauce will continue to thicken as it cools). If the sauce is too thick, add a little more water to loosen it.

Store in a sterilized sealed jar in the refrigerator and use within 1 month.

For a tropical twist, substitute the water with the same quantity of pineapple juice.

This Mexican inspired sauce has everything you want, with heat and a deep smoky undertone, it will transform anything it touches. Also makes a great barbecue marinade.

KALUA CHIPOTLE KETCHUP

3 x 400-g/14-oz. cans whole Italian tomatoes
3 tbsp dark soy sauce
3 tbsp muscovado sugar
1 tsp fish sauce
1 tbsp mirin
3 tbsp chipotle paste

MAKES 4 X 150-ML/ 5-OZ. BOTTLES

Put the whole tomatoes in a saucepan and heat gently. Add the soy sauce, muscovado sugar, fish sauce and mirin. Stir and bring the mixture to a very low simmer. Add in the chipotle paste and stir together. Continue to simmer for about 30 minutes until slightly reduced. Put everything in a blender and whizz to a smooth purée.

Sterilize the bottles by putting them in a boiling water bath, or microwave. When the bottles are ready, pour in the warm sauce and close the seals or lids. Store in a dry place, out of the light. Once open, keep the bottle in the fridge and use within one week.

A creamy, milder version of the chipotle ketchup, this one works on anything.

CHIPOTLE CREMA

1 tbsp Kalua Chipotle Ketchup (see opposite) or chipotle paste
3 tbsp double/heavy cream
1 tbsp good-quality mayonnaise

SERVES 4

Mix the ingredients together in a bowl.

The textural hero of so many dishes, these crispy fried onions add an irresistible crunch.

CRISPY SHALLOTS

4 shallots, finely sliced
vegetable oil
3 tbsp plain/all-purpose flour

MAKES ABOUT 350 ML/ SCANT 1½ CUPS

Shallow-fry the onions in a little oil over a medium heat for 5 minutes. Using a slotted spoon, remove the onions from the oil and drain on paper towels. Add a light coating of flour to the onions. Return the onions to the oil over a high heat and fry for about 1 minute again until golden.

An Asian-inspired version of a meatball pizza. The cooked pizza drizzled with sweet and savoury soy–lime glaze is served with a tangle of hot and sour crunchy kimchi salad.

KIMCHI & MEATBALL PIZZA WITH SOY-LIME GLAZE

Make the kimchi salad the day before if possible. Using a potato peeler, shave long strips from the cucumber avoiding the wet seeds. Do the same with the carrot and shred the spring onions. Mix the ginger, garlic, sugar, fish sauce, soy sauce and rice vinegar together in the bottom of a medium bowl. Throw in the vegetables and toss well to coat. Cover and refrigerate for as long as possible.

Put the pizza stone or baking sheets on the lower shelves of the oven. Preheat the oven to 220°C/200°C fan/425°F/gas 7 for at least 30 minutes.

Meanwhile, to make the meatballs, mix the milk with the egg and breadcrumbs and stir until absorbed. Add the pork, water chestnuts, chopped coriander, soy sauce, sesame oil and mix with your hands until well-combined. Take scant tablespoonfuls of the mix and roll each one into a small ball.

For the soy–lime glaze, stir together the soy sauce, sesame oil, lime juice and sugar with 4 tablespoons water in a small saucepan and boil for 2–3 minutes until slightly thickened. Set aside.

Roll or pull the pizza dough into two 35-cm/14-inch circles directly onto non-stick baking parchment. Slide these onto the rimless baking sheets. Scatter the tofu over the pizza bases, leaving a 1-cm/⅜-inch rim around the edge. Arrange the meatballs on top, then working quickly, open the oven door and slide paper and pizzas onto the hot pizza stone or baking sheets.

Bake for 5 minutes, then carefully slide out the baking parchment. Bake the pizzas for a further 10–15 minutes, or until the crust is golden and the meatballs cooked. Remove from the oven, drizzle with the glaze then divide the kimchi between the two pizzas, piling high. Finish with the coriander sprigs and eat immediately.

2 balls of ready-made pizza dough
200 g/7 oz. smoked firm tofu, grated

KIMCHI SALAD

1 small cucumber
1 large carrot
3 spring onions/scallions
25 g/1 oz. grated fresh ginger
2 garlic cloves, thinly sliced
2 tsp caster/granulated sugar
1–2 tsp fish sauce
1–2 tsp soy sauce
2 tsp rice vinegar
6–8 sprigs fresh coriander/ cilantro

MEATBALLS

2 tbsp milk
1 small egg, lightly beaten
4 tbsp fine dried breadcrumbs
350 g/12 oz. minced/ground pork
1 small can water chestnuts, drained and finely chopped
3 tbsp chopped fresh coriander/ cilantro
2 tsp soy sauce
1 tsp sesame oil

SOY–LIME GLAZE

4 tbsp soy sauce
2 tsp sesame oil
4 tbsp fresh lime juice
2 tbsp soft brown sugar

2 pizza stone or large, heavy baking sheets
2 rimless baking sheets

MAKES 2 THIN-CRUST PIZZAS (35 CM/14 INCHES)

There's no turning back once you've tried homemade maple-cured bacon, although you will need to prepare it a week in advance. When it's ready, just try to stop yourself frying up the whole lot and working your way through it with sticky fingers and guilty pleasure.

MAPLE-CURED BACON & TOMATO SANDWICH

Curing bacon at home takes a while, but it's really worth it. In a medium bowl, combine the salt, sugar and maple syrup. Rub the mixture over the pork belly on both sides. Place the pork in a large resealable plastic bag with a zip and seal tightly. Refrigerate and let cure for 7 days, turning once a day.

After 7 days, the bacon will be cured. Cut off a small piece and fry it to test the saltiness of the bacon. If the bacon doesn't taste too salty after being cooked, you are ready to proceed. If the bacon tastes too salty, soak the remaining pork belly in cold water for 1 hour.

Once the bacon is ready to cook, carefully slice it into strips of the desired thickness. Fry it for 3–4 minutes per side, until it reaches the crispiness that you like. Fry the eggs, if using.

Assemble the sandwiches with slices of sourdough bread, mayonnaise, eggs (if using), tomatoes, Cheddar cheese (if using), rocket, salt and pepper. Serve with sweet pickles and sweet potato fries.

8 slices sourdough bread
2 tbsp mayonnaise
4 fried eggs (optional)
8 tomato slices
4 slices Cheddar cheese (optional)
maple cured bacon (see below), 2 slices per sandwich
handful of rocket/arugula
sea salt and ground black pepper

MAPLE-CURED BACON

140 g/1 cup sea salt
400 g/2 cups brown sugar (preferably dark brown sugar)
320 g/1 cup pure maple syrup
2.25–4.5 kg/5–10 lbs. pork belly, washed and patted dry, with the skin left on

TO SERVE

your choice of pickles
sweet potato fries

SERVES 4

Schweppes

WINGS & RIBS

Honey and hot sauce – it doesn't get more on trend than that. A little bit of sugar and a little bit of spice go a long way in this timeless dish.

SWEET & SPICY WINGS

1.8 kg/4 lbs. chicken wings, halved at the joint, tips discarded
350 ml/1½ cups Louisiana-style hot sauce
175 g/¾ cup butter
340 g/1 cup runny honey
pinch of garlic salt
1 tsp cayenne pepper, or to taste
salt and freshly ground black pepper
blue cheese dressing or dip, to serve

SERVES 4

Preheat the oven to 180°C/160°C fan/350°F/gas 4. Grease the base of a large casserole or roasting dish.

Place the chicken in the dish and sprinkle with salt and pepper. Bake, uncovered, for 50–60 minutes in the preheated oven, turning the chicken over halfway through.

Combine the hot sauce, butter, honey, garlic salt, cayenne pepper and a pinch of black pepper in a medium saucepan. Place over a low-medium heat and melt the butter, stirring well. Increase the heat to medium-high and bring to the boil, continuing to stir, then reduce the heat to low-medium and cook for 40–45 minutes, stirring occasionally. The sauce will thicken to a syrupy consistency and will reduce by half.

When the chicken is cooked and the juices run clear when the thickest part is pierced to the bone, remove from the oven and drain off any cooking juices.

Pour half the sauce into the dish and toss the chicken. Return the wings to the oven for 5 minutes (or place under a preheated grill/ broiler).

Pour any remaining sauce over the chicken wings and serve them with a blue cheese dressing or dip.

Salt

This sweet and spicy combo uses harissa and honey for an unforgettable flavour. Baking, followed by grilling/broiling makes for perfect, fall-off-the-bone wings with wonderfully crispy skin.

HARISSA-HONEY HOT WINGS

1.8 kg/4 lbs. chicken wings, halved at the joints, tips removed
90 g/6 tbsp harissa
1 tbsp runny honey

SERVES 4–6

Preheat the oven to 190°C/170°C fan/375°F/gas 5. Line 2–3 baking sheets with foil.

Line up the wings on the baking sheets and bake for about 30 minutes until almost cooked through.

While the wings are baking, preheat the grill/broiler to high. When the wings have finished in the oven, grill/broil them for 3–5 minutes under the hot grill until the skin is crispy and the juices run clear when the thickest part is pierced to the bone.

Mix the harissa and honey together in a large bowl. Transfer the cooked wings to the bowl and stir to coat. The harissa mixture is thick, but the heat of the wings will soften it.

NOTE *These wings are fantastic served with Honey-Sriracha Sauce (see page 58) or a sriracha mayonnaise for dipping.*

Fried with a honey and sriracha coating, these wings are sweet and spicy, with the flavours playing off each other. The combination mixes east and west, with a little bit of the American South thrown in for good measure.

HONEY-SRIRACHA WINGS

vegetable or peanut oil, for frying

1.8 kg/4 lbs. chicken wings, halved at the joints, tips removed

225 g/1 cup unsalted butter, cut into 2.5-cm/1-in. pieces

180 g/¾ cup sriracha sauce

165 g/½ cup runny honey

1 tsp freshly ground black pepper

2 tsp kosher/flaked salt

dash of freshly squeezed lime juice

chopped fresh flat-leaf parsley

SERVES 4–6

Preheat the oven to 110°C/100°C fan/200°F/gas ¼.

Preheat the oil in a deep fryer to 180°C/350°F.

Fry the wings in batches for 10–12 minutes until crispy and golden brown and the juices run clear when the thickest part is pierced to the bone. Remove from the oil and place on 2–3 baking sheets in the preheated oven to keep warm.

While the wings are frying, melt the butter in a medium saucepan over a low heat. Add the sriracha, honey, pepper, salt and lime juice, stirring to combine. Keep warm over a low heat. When the sauce is combined, remove the wings from the oven.

Put the cooked wings in a large mixing bowl and toss with the honey-sriracha sauce. Garnish with parsley and serve with bread or crackers as preferred.

NOTE: *If you wish to make an accompanying sriracha-ranch dip, add 1 tablespoon sriracha to a ranch dressing.*

Fried first and then tossed in a sweet yet savoury caramel sauce, these wings have the perfect balance of delicate Asian flavours and seasoning. They are tastier still when served with a green onion dip on the side.

STICKY ASIAN CARAMEL WINGS

200 g/1 cup brown sugar
75 ml/⅓ cup fish sauce
75 ml/⅓ cup soy sauce
60 ml/¼ cup orange juice
60 ml/¼ cup freshly squeezed lime juice
1.8 kg/4 lbs. chicken wings, halved at the joints, tips removed
vegetable oil, for frying
egg-fried rice and an Asian slaw, to serve (optional)

GREEN ONION DIP

250 ml/1 cup sour cream
225 g/1 cup mayonnaise
50 g/½ cup finely chopped spring onions/scallions
30 g/½ cup finely chopped fresh flat-leaf parsley
2 garlic cloves, finely chopped
1 tsp Dijon mustard

SERVES 4–6

First, make the dip. Mix all the ingredients in a blender until smooth. Cover and refrigerate until ready to serve.

Place the sugar in a medium saucepan with 60 ml/¼ cup water and bring to the boil. Continue to boil and swirl (don't stir) for 6–7 minutes so the sugar caramelizes evenly.

Combine the fish sauce, soy sauce, orange juice and lime juice with 60 ml/¼ cup water in a small bowl. Once the caramel has turned a golden amber colour, slowly pour the fish sauce mixture into the pan and return to the boil. Continue to boil for 7 minutes until the sauce is well combined, then remove the sauce from the heat and keep warm.

Meanwhile, preheat the oil in the deep fat fryer to 180°C/350°F.

Fry the chicken wings in batches for about 10 minutes until cooked through and the juices run clear when the thickest part is pierced to the bone. Remove and drain on paper towels. Place in a large bowl, pour the caramel sauce over the wings and toss. Serve with the green onion dip on the side.

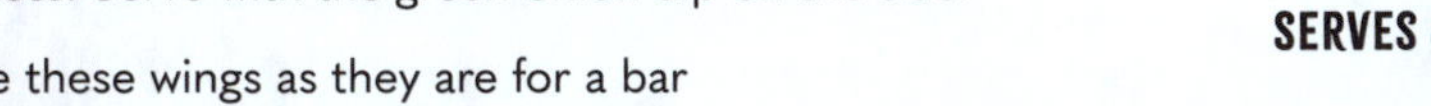

Serve these wings as they are for a bar bite or add rice and an Asian-style slaw to create a more substantial plateful.

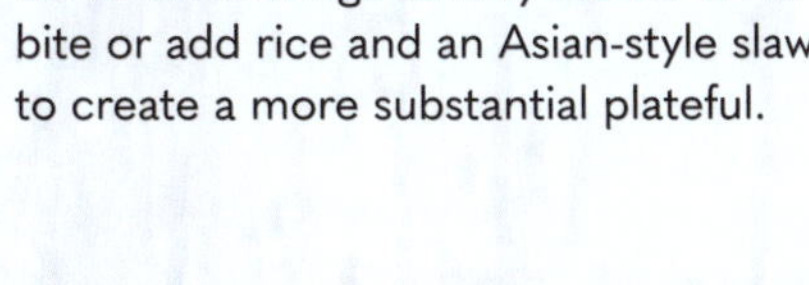

These oven-fried, Asian-inspired chicken wings are flavoured with reduced sake, teriyaki sauce, ginger and chilli flakes/hot red pepper flakes. A teri-sake infusion!

SAKE WINGS

250 ml/1 cup soy sauce
120 ml/½ cup sake, dry sherry or dry white wine
3 tbsp very finely chopped fresh ginger
1½ tbsp finely chopped garlic
200 g/1 cup sugar
1½ tsp chilli flakes/ hot red pepper flakes
100 g/1 cup thinly sliced spring onions/scallions, (white and green parts), plus extra for garnish
3½ tbsp rice vinegar
3 tbsp cornflour/cornstarch
2 tbsp toasted sesame seeds
1.8 kg/4 lbs. chicken wings, halved at the joints, tips removed

PLUM DIPPING SAUCE

1.3 kg/3 lbs. plums, pitted and chopped
4 garlic cloves, finely chopped
1 tbsp finely chopped fresh ginger
1 small onion, finely chopped
200 g/1 cup brown sugar
2 tbsp teriyaki sauce
1 tsp sesame oil
2 tbsp soy sauce
½ tsp crushed dried chilli
freshly squeezed juice of 1 lemon
2 tbsp cornflour/cornstarch

SERVES 4–6

First, make the plum dipping sauce. Place all the ingredients except the cornflour in a medium saucepan with 475 ml/ 2 cups water. Bring to the boil, then reduce the heat and simmer for about 30 minutes. Remove from the heat. Mix the cornflour with 1 tablespoon water, then pour into a blender with the plum mixture. Blend until combined. Pour back into the pan and cook over a medium-low heat until the mixture thickens to the desired consistency. Set aside to cool, then refrigerate until needed.

In a small saucepan, whisk together the soy sauce, sake (or sherry or white wine), ginger, garlic, sugar, chilli flakes, spring onions, vinegar and cornflour with 3 tablespoons water. Set the pan over a medium heat and bring to the boil, whisking constantly (the mixture will be very thick). Let cool.

Preheat the oven to 190°C/170°C fan/375°F/gas 5. Grease 2–3 baking sheets with cooking spray or vegetable oil.

Add the sauce mixture to a large bowl with the wings and mix well. Arrange the wings in a single layer on the baking sheets and pour over any leftover sauce. Bake in the preheated oven for 30 minutes. Stir and turn the wings over in the sauce, then bake for a further 20 minutes. Stir and turn the wings again and bake for a final 10 minutes, or until the chicken is tender and the juices run clear when the thickest part is pierced to the bone, and the sauce is thick and shiny. Transfer to a serving platter. Spoon some of the extra sauce over, then sprinkle with the sesame seeds and spring onions.

These sweet and spicy Chinese chicken wings are sautéed in a pan for tender meat and combined with a hot and sticky sauce for the most lip-smacking results.

KUNG PAO WINGS

120 ml/½ cup white wine
120 ml/½ cup soy sauce
4 tbsp sesame oil,
50 g/½ cup cornflour/ cornstarch, dissolved in 120 ml/½ cup water
1.8 kg/4 lbs. chicken wings, halved at the joints, tips removed
85 g/3 oz. hot chilli paste
1½ tbsp distilled white vinegar
3 tbsp brown sugar
4 spring onions/scallions, chopped, plus extra to garnish
4 garlic cloves, finely chopped
450-g/16-oz. can water chestnuts, drained and sliced
100 g/1 cup chopped peanuts
1 fresh red chilli/chile, sliced, to garnish

SERVES 4–6

Combine 4 tablespoons of the wine, 4 tablespoons of the soy sauce, 2 tablespoons of the sesame oil and 4 tablespoons of the cornflour mixture in a bowl and mix together. Place the wings in a large, resealable plastic bag. Add the marinade, seal the bag and toss to coat. Place in the refrigerator to marinate overnight, or for at least 4 hours.

In a small bowl, combine the remaining wine, soy sauce, oil and cornflour mixture with the chilli paste, vinegar and sugar. Mix together and add the chopped onion, garlic, water chestnuts and peanuts. Transfer the mixture to a medium frying pan/skillet and heat the sauce slowly until aromatic.

Meanwhile, remove the chicken from the marinade and sauté in a second large frying pan until the meat is cooked through and the juices run clear when the thickest part is pierced to the bone. When the sauce is aromatic, add the sautéed chicken to it and let it simmer together until the sauce thickens, then serve immediately. Garnish with the sliced chilli and spring onion.

These crisp, herby wings are the perfect pairing to a sticky caramel dip. A match made in heaven!

EXTRA-CRUNCHY CRUMBED WINGS

1.8 kg/4 lbs. chicken wings, halved at the joints, tips removed

500 ml/2 cups buttermilk (optional)

4 large eggs, beaten

100 g/¾ cup sesame seeds

100 g/¾ cup plain/all-purpose flour

1 tbsp coarse salt

½ tsp cayenne pepper

250 g/4 cups fresh breadcrumbs

4 garlic cloves, finely chopped

SOY-CARAMEL DIP

75 g/⅓ cup sugar

4–5 large shallots, chopped

1 garlic clove, finely chopped

½ tbsp finely chopped fresh ginger

3 tbsp soy sauce

3 tbsp rice vinegar (not seasoned)

2 tbsp cornflour/cornstarch

1 tbsp freshly squeezed lemon juice (optional)

SERVES 4–6

If using buttermilk, put the wings and buttermilk in a medium bowl and cover. Refrigerate overnight, or for at least 4 hours.

Make the soy-caramel dip. Cook the sugar in a large, dry, heavy-based saucepan over a medium-high heat, undisturbed, until it melts around the edges and begins to turn a perfect golden colour. Add the shallots (use caution as the caramel will bubble up and steam vigorously) and cook for 45 seconds, stirring, until the shallots shrink and become fragrant. Add the garlic and ginger and cook, stirring, for 30 seconds. Stir in the soy sauce, vinegar and 335 ml/1⅓ cups water and simmer for 1 minute, stirring, until any hardened caramel has dissolved. The sauce will become a rich auburn colour.

Mix the cornflour with 2 tablespoons water until smooth, then stir into the sauce and simmer for 2 minutes, stirring occasionally. Remove from the heat and plunge the pan into a sink of cold water to stop the caramel cooking. If using lemon juice, stir it in now. Cover the sauce and keep warm.

Preheat the oven to 190°C/170°C fan/375°F/gas 5. Line 2–3 baking sheets with baking parchment, or grease with oil.

Remove the wings from the buttermilk and discard. Place the wings in a large bowl, add the eggs and toss to coat.

Combine the sesame seeds, flour, salt, cayenne pepper, breadcrumbs and garlic in a small bowl. Dip each wing into the sesame mixture to fully coat. Place the coated wings side by side on the baking sheets.

Bake in the preheated oven for 30 minutes, then increase the oven temperature to 200°C/180°C fan/400°F/gas 6. Cook for a further 20–30 minutes until the wings are golden brown and sizzling, and the juices run clear when the thickest part is pierced to the bone. Remove the wings from the baking sheets and serve with the soy-caramel dip.

These oven-baked teriyaki wings are marinated in a tangy pineapple-based teriyaki sauce. Serve with green onion–ranch dip for added flavour.

STICKY TERIYAKI WINGS

350 ml/1½ cups soy sauce
300 g/1½ cups sugar
175 ml/¾ cup pineapple juice
120 ml/¾ cup vegetable oil
2 garlic cloves, finely chopped
1½ tbsp finely chopped fresh ginger
1.8 kg/4 lbs. chicken wings, halved at the joints, tips removed

GREEN ONION–RANCH DIP

225 ml/1 cup sour cream
225 g/1 cup mayonnaise
35 g/½ cup finely chopped spring onions/scallions
1 tbsp finely chopped fresh flat-leaf parsley
1 garlic clove, finely chopped
1 tsp Dijon mustard

SERVES 4–6

First make the dipping sauce by combining all the ingredients in a blender and whizzing until smooth. Transfer to a small bowl, cover and refrigerate until ready to serve.

Combine the soy sauce, sugar, pineapple juice, vegetable oil, garlic and ginger in a large bowl with 350 ml/1½ cups water. Stir until the sugar has dissolved. Pour the marinade into a large resealable plastic bag. Add the wings to the bag and marinate in the refrigerator overnight or for at least 4 hours.

Preheat the oven to 180°C/160°C fan/350°F/gas 5. Line 2–3 baking sheets with foil.

Remove the chicken from the marinade and arrange on the baking sheets. Brush with the remaining marinade. Bake in the preheated oven for about 1 hour, or until the juices run clear when the thickest part is pierced to the bone.

NOTE *Serve these wings with the green onion-ranch dip for a bar bite but add cooked rice noodles and wilted Chinese cabbage/pak choi for a more substantial plateful.*

Jerk seasoning mixed with a sticky rum sauce provides the perfect level of heat plus sweetness in these irresistible wings.

JERK WINGS WITH STICKY RUM SAUCE

500 g/1 lb. 2 oz. chicken wings
30 g/1 oz. Greek yogurt
60 g/2 oz. jerk seasoning
½ bunch of fresh thyme, leaves removed

STICKY RUM SAUCE

4 garlic cloves, peeled
¼ onion, peeled
50–100 g/¼–½ cup granulated sugar
100 ml/3½ fl oz. tomato ketchup
75 ml/⅓ cup malt brown vinegar
50 ml/scant ¼ cup dark soy sauce
50 ml/3 tbsp honey
1 tsp English mustard
1–2 tbsp good-quality cornflour or plain/all-purpose flour
125 ml/½ cup white rum

TO SERVE

baby leaf spinach
pineapple chunks
roasted peppers
snipped fresh chives

SERVES 2–4

Preheat the oven to 245°C/220°C fan/475°F/gas 9.

Place the wings in a small roasting pan and rub all over with the yogurt. Cover the tin and place in the fridge for 15–20 minutes.

Remove the tin from the fridge and season the wings vigorously with the jerk seasoning and thyme by rubbing them into the skin. Add about 60 ml/¼ cup water to the pan and cover the roasting pan tightly with foil. Bake in the preheated oven for 20 minutes, or until the wings begin to scorch.

Meanwhile, make the sauce. Put the garlic, onion, sugar and 125ml/½ cup water in a food processor and pulse until combined. Transfer to a saucepan. Add the ketchup, soy sauce, honey, mustard and cornflour and combine with a whisk. Bring to the boil and continue boiling until the sauce thickens. If the sauce is too thin, add a little more cornflour; if it is too thick add a little more water. Leave the sauce to cool.

After 20 minutes roasting, drain the cooking juices from the wings and add this stock and the rum to the cooled sauce and whisk together.

Pour the sauce generously over the wings, saving some sauce for serving. Cover the roasting pan with foil and return to the oven for a further 10 minutes, then remove the foil and roast the wings, uncovered, for a final 10 minutes until slightly charred.

Serve the chicken wings, alongside any leftover sauce, on a bed of fresh spinach leaves with pineapple, roasted peppers and garnish with chives.

Supermalt is a malty non-alcoholic drink popular in Nigerian households. Its combined sweetness and maltiness works brilliantly with the oven baked wings, with some added heat from the hot honey glaze.

MIGHTY SUPERMALT WINGS

Preheat the oven to 200°C/180°C fan/400°F/gas 6.

Toss the chicken wings with the olive oil, chicken stock powder, salt, black pepper, garlic powder, onion powder and smoked paprika, making sure the wings are evenly coated.

Arrange the wings on a baking sheet lined with foil, making sure they are not overcrowded.

Bake in the preheated oven for 45–50 minutes, or until the wings are golden brown and crispy all over, flipping them halfway through the cooking time.

Now, make the hot honey glaze. In a small saucepan over a medium heat, combine the honey, chopped Scotch bonnet, Supermalt and garlic. Bring the mixture to a simmer, stirring occasionally, and continue simmering for 5–7 minutes, or until the sauce thickens slightly – it should have a glossy shine to it.

Once the wings are done baking, put them in a large clean bowl. Pour the hot honey glaze over the wings and toss them until evenly coated.

Garnish with sesame seeds and spring onions, if liked, and serve the wings hot.

1.5 kg/3¼ lb. chicken wings, split at the joint, tips discarded

3 tbsp olive oil

1 tbsp Jumbo chicken stock powder

1 tbsp salt

2 tbsp freshly ground black pepper

3 tsp garlic powder

1 tsp onion powder

3 tbsp smoked paprika

sesame seeds and chopped spring onions/scallions, to garnish (optional)

HOT HONEY GLAZE

60 g/¼ cup organic honey

½ Scotch bonnet chilli/chile, finely chopped

120 g/½ cup Original Supermalt

2 garlic cloves, crushed/ minced

SERVES 3–4

Ideal for that movie night or relaxed meal at the weekend. Your friends and family will love you for cooking this, but beware, things will get messy! Great served with a fruity slaw.

STICKY RUM RIBS

2-kg/4½-lb. pork ribs
1 tbsp sea salt
2 tbsp brown sugar

EARTH SPICE RUB
2 tbsp smoked paprika
2 tsp black peppercorns
1 tsp each cayenne pepper, ground turmeric, fennel seeds, ground cumin, celery seeds, dried oregano and sea salt

MARINADE
4 tbsp runny honey
3 tbsp soy sauce
2 tbsp sesame oil
100 ml/⅓ cup dark rum

GLAZE
3 tbsp treacle/molasses
2 tbsp soy sauce
100 ml/⅓ cup apple cider vinegar
6 whole allspice berries
1 tsp ground ginger
2 tbsp freshly chopped thyme leaves
4 tbsp runny honey
200 ml/¾ cup orange juice
1 cinnamon stick
100 ml/⅓ cup dark rum

baking pan, lined with foil with a grill rack inside

SERVES 4–6

For the earth spice rub, grind all the spices and herbs together in a food processor. Stir in the sea salt and set aside.

Prepare a large plastic fridge bag or other container that will fit the ribs. (If your racks of ribs are too large, you can cut them in half along one of the bones, but try not to disassemble them too much, as they will cook best left as whole as possible.) Rub the ribs with the salt, sugar and earth spice seasoning.

Stir together all of the marinade ingredients in a small bowl. Place the ribs in the plastic bag or container, then cover evenly with the marinade and refrigerate for at least 2 hours or overnight.

Preheat the oven to 150°C/130°C fan/300°F/gas 2.

Arrange the ribs on the grill rack in the prepared baking pan and cover them with foil. Cook in the preheated oven for 2 hours, turning the meat over halfway through.

Meanwhile, make the glaze. Combine all the ingredients, except the rum, in a saucepan and bring to the boil. Reduce the heat and simmer gently for 30–45 minutes, until the glaze has thickened. Stir the rum into the glaze, simmer for 1 minute, then remove from the heat and keep warm.

Once 2 hours have passed, uncover the ribs, flip again, and brush with some of the glaze. Put them back in the oven, uncovered, for 1 more hour. Flip and re-glaze the ribs at the final 30-minute mark.

Remove the ribs from the oven and place on a chopping board to rest for 5–10 minutes. Cut the ribs into portions along the bone so that each individual rib has plenty of meat and place on a large platter. Serve with a bowl of the remaining warm glaze on the side, for dipping.

This is such a showstopper. The richness in flavour and sticky marinade combined with fall off the bone meat – there is nothing not to like if you love pork.

GUINNESS PORK RIBS

2 large racks of pork ribs or 4 smaller ones (weighing around 1.8–2.7 kg/4–6 lb. in total)
juice of 1 large lemon
2 tbsp Jumbo chicken stock powder (or 2 tsp each of salt and dried thyme)
480 ml/2 cups Nigerian Guinness stout
1 tbsp soft dark brown sugar
120 ml/½ cup soy sauce
1 large garlic clove, crushed/ minced
2 tbsp Dijon mustard
2 tbsp smoked paprika
2 tbsp garlic powder
1 tbsp onion salt
4 tbsp Worcestershire sauce
6 tbsp barbecue sauce
salt and freshly ground black pepper

SERVES 4–6

Preheat the oven to 150°C/130°C fan/300°F/gas 2.

Wash the pork in a bowl with the fresh lemon juice.

Grab a knife and clean off any excess fat and remove the membrane from the back of the ribs (if present). Rinse under running water, then pat dry. Season the ribs generously with the chicken stock powder.

Mix the Nigerian Guinness, brown sugar, soy sauce, garlic, Dijon mustard, smoked paprika, garlic powder, onion salt, Worcestershire sauce and barbecue sauce together in a bowl.

Place the seasoned ribs in a large oven tray or baking dish, meaty side up. Pour the Guinness mixture over the ribs, ensuring that they are evenly coated. Leave a cheeky bit of sauce behind so you can baste the ribs as they cook. Cover the oven tray tightly with foil.

Place the ribs in the preheated oven and bake for 3 hours, opening and basting every hour or so, until the meat is ready to fall off the bone.

Remove the foil from the oven tray or baking dish, increase the oven temperature to 200°C/180°C fan/400°F/gas 6, and return the ribs to the oven for 20 minutes to caramelize.

Remove the ribs from the oven and pour the sauce in the tray into a gravy boat to serve alongside the ribs. Serve piping hot.

Everyone has their own preference when it comes to barbecue ribs. Some like them rubbed with spices with no sauce, while others smother sauce all over. Chicago-style ribs involve both a rub and a sauce; for best results they're first grilled slowly, then cooked in the oven to make them really tender.

CHICAGO-STYLE BABY BACK RIBS

Mix the dry rub ingredients together in a bowl. Rub the ribs with the spice mix and let sit for 30 minutes.

Preheat a charcoal grill or barbecue. Cook the ribs over an indirect medium heat for 10–15 minutes.

Preheat an oven to 120°C/100°C fan/250°F/gas 1/2.

Add about 1.25 cm/1/2 inch water to an oblong baking pan and place a grill rack into the pan. Place the ribs on the rack and cover tightly with foil. Bake for about 1½ hours, then remove from the oven.

Mix all the sauce ingredients together in a cup and spread over the ribs, reserving some to serve. Cover tightly again with foil and set aside for 15 minutes before serving. Serve along with the extra sauce.

2 racks of baby back ribs

DRY RUB

1 tbsp paprika
1 tsp celery salt
1 tsp dark brown sugar
1 tsp garlic powder
1/4 tsp mustard powder
1/4 tsp dried thyme
1/4 tsp ground white pepper
1/4 tsp cayenne pepper

BARBECUE SAUCE

340 g/2½ cups tomato ketchup
115 g/1/2 cup golden syrup/ molasses
125 ml/1/2 cup apple cider vinegar
125 ml/1/2 cup water
1 tsp granulated sugar
1/2 tsp salt
1/2 tsp ground black pepper

charcoal grill or barbecue

SERVES 4

Gochujang is a red pepper paste used in Korean cooking. It comes in varying degrees of heat, so make sure to check the label and choose something to suit your taste buds. These ribs are great for the barbecue; serve them with an Asian coleslaw or kimchi.

KOREAN STICKY RIBS

Lay the ribs in a single layer in a ceramic baking dish.

Put all the marinade ingredients in a blender and process until smooth. Pour over the ribs and sprinkle with the spring onions/scallions and sesame seeds. Cover and refrigerate for 6–24 hours. Remove the ribs from the fridge and bring to room temperature.

Heat a grill/broiler or barbecue to a medium–high heat. Place the ribs on the rack and cook for 5 minutes, then turn over and cook for another 5 minutes. Transfer to a warm plate and tent with foil. Rest for 10 minutes.

Put the remaining marinade in a small saucepan and bring to the boil, then reduce the heat and simmer for 5 minutes. To serve, pour the marinade into a bowl and serve alongside the ribs.

8 Korean-style beef ribs, 1 cm/½ inch thick
3 spring onions/scallions, finely sliced
2 tbsp black sesame seeds

MARINADE

60 ml/¼ cup soy sauce
60 ml/¼ cup toasted sesame oil
140 g/½ cup orange-blossom honey
2 heaped tbsp gochujang or sambal oelek (Asian chilli/chile paste)
1 tbsp fish sauce
4 garlic cloves, bashed
2 Serrano chillies/chiles, roughly chopped
2 tsp cracked rainbow peppercorns
½ tsp sea salt

SERVES 4–6

This mouthwatering fusion recipe has been adapted slightly to include English mustard as an ingredient. Your guests will be crazy in love for these succulent spareribs – they will polish off every last shred of meat. This marinade can also be used for chicken thighs, drumsticks and pork chops.

VIETNAMESE BARBECUE SPARERIBS

In a bowl, mix together all the ingredients (except the meat) to make a marinade. Add the meat and rub the marinade in well. Cover and refrigerate for at least 30 minutes.

Preheat the oven to 200°C/180°C fan/400°F/gas 6.

Transfer the meat to a roasting pan and roast in the preheated oven for 45 minutes or until cooked through and the juices run clear when you stick a knife in. The meat can also be grilled on a barbecue, in which case times will vary, so check that it's cooked through before serving.

Scatter the sesame seeds over the top before serving, if using.

4 Asian shallots, finely chopped

1 large garlic clove, finely chopped

4 tsp English mustard

4 tsp soy sauce

6 tbsp hoisin sauce

1 tbsp Sriracha chilli sauce

1 tsp honey

800 g/1¾ lbs. pork spareribs (or chicken wings, thighs, drumsticks or chops)

1 tsp sesame seeds, to garnish (optional)

SERVES 4–6

Spare ribs, braised in an aromatic tomato ginger sauce, make a rich, flavourful dish. Serve with steamed rice and a vegetable side dish, such as blanched Chinese greens.

TOMATO GINGER SPARE RIBS

450 g/1 lb. ripe tomatoes
2 tbsp oil, plus extra for shallow frying
2 onions, peeled and finely chopped
2 garlic cloves, peeled and chopped
2 x 5-cm/2-inch pieces of fresh ginger, peeled and finely chopped
1 tsp Chinese five-spice powder
1 tbsp sherry or rice wine
2 tsp dark soy sauce
1 tbsp tomato purée/paste
1 tbsp brown sugar
300 ml/1¼ cups chicken stock
12 pork spare ribs (about 1.2 kg/2½ lbs.)

SERVES 4

Begin by scalding the tomatoes. Pour boiling water over the ripe tomatoes in a heatproof bowl. Set aside for 1 minute, then drain and carefully peel off the skin using a sharp knife. Roughly chop, reserving any juices, and set aside.

Heat the oil in a frying pan/skillet set over a medium heat. Add the onions, garlic and ginger, and fry gently, stirring often, for 2–3 minutes until softened.

Mix the five-spice powder with 1 tablespoon cold water to form a paste. Add this to the pan with the onions, garlic and ginger, and stir in, frying briefly. Add the sherry and cook, stirring often, for 1 minute. Add the chopped tomatoes, soy sauce, tomato purée, sugar and chicken stock and mix together. Bring to the boil and cook, stirring occasionally, for 10–15 minutes, until the sauce has thickened and reduced.

Preheat the oven to 200°C/180°C fan/400°F/gas 6.

Heat enough oil for shallow frying in a large frying pan/skillet set over a medium heat. Cook the spare ribs in batches and brown on all sides. Transfer the ribs to a roasting pan and pour over the tomato sauce to coat.

Bake in the preheated oven for 45 minutes until the ribs are cooked through. Remove and serve hot.

BOWL FOOD

Crispy 5-spice Tofu with Sweet & Sour Chilli Sauce

Beef Dolsot Bibimbap

Bibimbap Salad with Seared Beef

Chicken Teriyaki with Lime on Quinoa Rice

Spicy Barbecue Korean Beef Rice Bowl

Gochujang-Glazed Mushroom & Wholegrain Rice Bowls

Barbecue Pork Noodle Bowls with Dipping Sauce

Banh Mi Rice Bowl

Prawn, Crab & Tamarind Rice Noodles

Sticky Aubergine Poke with Sour Carrot Salad

Sweet Chilli Pork Belly & Noodles

Sweet & Sour Orange Chicken with Pineapple Fried Rice

The crispy outside of deep-fried tofu houses a soft and tender centre that is ideally suited to absorb the aromatics of Chinese 5-spice powder and the sweet and sticky sauce. This chilli/chili sauce keeps well in the fridge and is also great with all types of foods – try with burgers, sandwiches or even just simple grilled fish and chicken.

CRISPY 5-SPICE TOFU WITH SWEET & SOUR CHILLI SAUCE

500 g/1 lb. 2 oz. firm tofu, drained
40 g/4¾ tbsp self-raising/rising flour
1 tsp Chinese 5-spice powder
½ tsp sea salt
a pinch of cayenne pepper
sunflower oil, for deep-frying

CHILLI SAUCE

6 large red chillies/chiles
4 garlic cloves, roughly chopped
2 tsp grated root ginger
2 tsp fish sauce
100 ml/⅓ cup plus 1 tbsp rice wine vinegar
100 g/½ cup granulated sugar

TO SERVE

cooked jasmine rice
2 carrots, shredded
1 cucumber, deseeded and shredded
50 g/2 oz. beansprouts, trimmed
4 spring onions/scallions, shredded
a few sprigs each of Thai basil, mint and coriander/cilantro

SERVES 6

To make the sauce, put the chillies, garlic and ginger in a food processor and blitz until fairly smooth, then transfer to a saucepan with the fish sauce, vinegar and sugar. Bring to the boil and simmer gently for 10 minutes or until thickened with a jam-like consistency. Spoon directly into a sterilized jar, seal with a vinegar-safe lid and set aside until required.

Cut the tofu into 2-cm/¾-inch cubes. Sift the flour into a bowl and stir in the Chinese 5-spice, sea salt and cayenne pepper until evenly combined. Toss the tofu pieces in the spiced flour mixture until evenly coated.

Pour enough oil into a heavy-based deep saucepan to come no more than a third of the way up the sides and heat until the oil reaches 180°C/350°F. As soon as the oil reaches temperature, very carefully lower the tofu into the hot oil (working in batches if needed) and cook for about 2 minutes until crisp and golden.

Serve with bowls of jasmine rice topped with the tofu, chilli sauce and the vegetables and herbs.

A dolsot bowl is a stone (or earthenware) bowl that is preheated before the food is added to serve. It allows the rice at the bottom of the dish to crisp slightly, adding a bite of texture. Use any heatproof bowls you have.

BEEF DOLSOT BIBIMBAP

Place the beef in a bowl and add the apple juice, garlic, soy sauce and honey. Stir well and leave to marinate for at least 1 hour. Remove the beef from the marinade and dry well, reserving the marinade juices.

Cook the rice according to the packet instructions. Keep warm.

Preheat the oven to 220°C/200°C fan/425°F/gas 7. Put two heatproof bowls into the oven to heat.

Make the bibimbap sauce. Place all the ingredients in a bowl with 1 tablespoon cold water and stir well. Set aside.

Prepare the vegetables. Heat the sesame oil in a frying pan/skillet and stir-fry the garlic and spring onions for 2 minutes until softened. Stir in the sesame seeds, then take off the heat.

Blanch the spinach for 30 seconds in boiling water. Drain and squeeze dry. Place in a bowl and keep warm.

Heat the vegetable oil in a frying pan and stir-fry the carrot for 2 minutes until lightly golden. Transfer to a bowl. Repeat with the mushrooms for 2–3 minutes until softened. Transfer to a bowl. Divide the spring onion mixture equally between the vegetables, stir well and keep warm.

Cook the beef. Heat the vegetable oil in a heavy-based frying pan and, when hot, add the marinated beef. Stir-fry for 2 minutes until browned. Add the marinade juices, simmer and then remove from the heat.

Carefully remove the hot bowls from the oven and add 1 teaspoon sesame oil to each one. Divide the cooked rice between the bowls and press down with a spatula. Top each one with the beef, the vegetables and bibimbap sauce.

300 g/10½ oz. beef fillet, sliced thinly
60 ml/¼ cup apple juice
2 garlic cloves, crushed
2 tbsp dark soy sauce
1 tbsp clear honey
200 g/7 oz. Japanese rice
1 tbsp vegetable oil
2 tsp sesame oil, plus extra to serve

BIBIMBAP SAUCE

4 tbsp gochujang
2 tbsp caster/granulated sugar
1 tbsp light soy sauce
1 tbsp sesame oil

VEGETABLES

1 tbsp sesame oil
2 garlic cloves, finely chopped
2 spring onions/scallions, thinly sliced
1 tbsp sesame seeds, toasted
60 g/2 oz. spinach leaves, stalks removed
1 tbsp vegetable oil
1 carrot, cut into matchsticks
60 g/2 oz. shiitake, oyster or enoki mushrooms, sliced

SERVES 2

Traditionally, bibimbap is a Korean hot rice dish but its versatility easily allows for it to be served as a salad, where the rice is cooked and cooled and then topped with a selection of vegetables, seared meats and a dressing. This dish is loosely based on a Thai seared beef salad, albeit with a Korean slant.

BIBIMBAP SALAD WITH SEARED BEEF

300 g/10½ oz. beef fillet steak
400 g/14 oz. cooked white long grain rice, cooled and chilled
2 handfuls of salad leaves or micro herbs
½ cucumber, thickly sliced
100 g/3½ oz. shelled edamame beans
50 g/1¾ oz. cherry tomatoes, halved
1 avocado, sliced

MARINADE

½ tbsp gochujang
1 tbsp sake
½ tsp gochugaru
1 tbsp light soy sauce
½ tbsp dark soy sauce
½ tbsp soft brown sugar

SESAME DRESSING

3 tbsp white sesame seeds
3 tbsp white wine vinegar
3 tbsp light soy sauce
3 tbsp soft brown sugar
1 tbsp sesame oil

SERVES 2

Start by making the marinade. Place all the ingredients in a bowl with 2 tablespoons cold water and stir well. Add the beef fillet and marinate for at least 1 hour, or overnight. Remove the beef from the marinade.

Make the dressing. Pound the seeds in a pestle and mortar or spice grinder to form a smooth paste. Gradually stir in the vinegar and remaining ingredients. Taste and adjust the amount of soy, sugar and vinegar to meet your required taste.

Heat a griddle or heavy-based frying pan/skillet over a high heat. Add the marinated beef and chargrill for 30–60 seconds on each side, depending on how rare you like your beef. Remove from the pan and set aside to rest for 5 minutes.

Divide the cooked rice between bowls and add the salad leaves, sliced cucumber, edamame, tomatoes and avocado. Slice the beef and divide between the bowls adding any juices. Drizzle over the sesame dressing and serve.

Ready-made bottles of the sweet, soy-based glaze that you can use to marinate your chicken are easily available, but nothing beats the taste of a homemade teriyaki sauce. Add a squeeze of lime juice for an extra fragrant twist.

CHICKEN TERIYAKI WITH LIME ON QUINOA RICE

1 tbsp vegetable oil
2 leeks, chopped into 2-cm/3/4-inch lengths
500 g/1 lb. 2 oz. boneless skin-on chicken thigh fillets, diced into bite-sized pieces
4 tbsp potato starch or cornflour/cornstarch

TERIYAKI SAUCE WITH LIME

3 tabsp soy sauce
3 tbsp mirin
1 tbsp soft light brown sugar
1 tbsp sake
1 tbsp lime juice and grated zest from 1/2 lime

TO SERVE

800 g/6 cups cooked Japanese rice and quinoa, to serve
toasted white and black sesame seeds
yuzu kosho chilli/chili paste, to serve (optional)

SERVES 4

First, make the teriyaki sauce. In a small bowl, mix together the soy sauce, mirin, brown sugar, sake, lime juice and zest, stirring until the sugar has dissolved. Set aside.

Add 1/2 tablespoon of the vegetable oil to a frying pan/skillet over a medium heat. Add the leeks and fry until lightly browned on each side. Remove them from the pan and set aside.

Place the chicken pieces in a bowl and lightly toss with the potato starch or cornflour to coat evenly all over.

Add the remaining 1/2 tablespoon vegetable oil to the same frying pan/skillet and fry the chicken, skin-side down, for 2 minutes until browned. Remove the pan from the heat briefly and remove the excess chicken fat by tilting the pan to the side and carefully soaking up the fat with 1–2 paper towels (taking care not to actually touch the surface of the hot pan with your hand).

Turn the chicken pieces over and cook for 2 minutes on the other side.

Add the leeks back into the pan, then pour over the teriyaki sauce, stirring to coat the chicken and leeks evenly. Simmer for 4–5 minutes over a medium-high heat until the sauce has thickened.

Divide the cooked rice and quinoa between serving bowls, then add the teriyaki chicken. Sprinkle with toasted sesame seeds and serve with yuzu kosho chilli paste, if you want some extra heat.

Barbecuing is highly prized in Korean cooking and there are a host of different barbecued classics. Here beef short ribs are slow-cooked for several hours to render them tender. If you prefer to use a different cut of beef, you could use brisket or chuck steak. You will need to begin this recipe a day ahead.

SPICY BARBECUE KOREAN BEEF RICE BOWL

Combine the marinade ingredients in a bowl. Add the beef ribs, coat well and marinate overnight.

The next day, heat the oven to 150°C/130°C fan/300°F/gas 2. Line a roasting pan with baking paper and lay the ribs on top. Cover the whole tin with foil and bake for 3 hours, or until the meat is falling from the bone. Don't be tempted to remove the beef from the oven until it is really tender.

Make the chogochujang sauce. Dry fry the sesame seeds in a small frying pan/skillet until evenly toasted. Transfer to a pestle and mortar (or spice grinder) and pound to a rough paste. Place in a bowl and stir in the gochujang, vinegar, soy sauce, honey and sesame oil until smooth, then add the spring onion and garlic and stir well. Set aside.

Cook the rice according to packet instructions. Keep warm.

Once the beef is tender. Heat a barbecue until hot or alternatively use a conventional grill/broiler heated to its highest setting. Cook the ribs for 10 minutes until really charred all over.

Arrange the rice in bowls. Top with the beef and all the garnishes. Serve with the sauce to drizzle or dip.

1 kg/2 lb. beef short ribs
400 g/2¼ cups Korean or Japanese sticky rice

MARINADE

3 garlic cloves
3 tbsp soft brown sugar
4 tbsp dark soy sauce
2 tbsp sesame oil
1 tbsp chilli/chili sauce
1 tbsp freshly grated root ginger
2 star anise, lightly bashed

CHOGOCHUJANG SAUCE

1 tbsp sesame seeds
1–2 tsp gochujang
2 tbsp rice wine vinegar
2 tbsp dark soy sauce
1 tbsp clear honey
2 tsp sesame oil
1 spring onion/scallion, finely chopped
1 garlic clove, crushed

GARNISHES

carrots, shredded
avocado, thinly sliced
beansprouts, trimmed
red onions, thinly sliced
cucumber, shredded
perilla leaves

SERVES 4

There is something very appealing about bowl food. Here, classic Korean flavourings – including gochujang (Korean chilli paste), aromatic root ginger and pungent garlic – transform delicate, fresh exotic mushrooms into a piquant, flavourful topping for a bowl of rice.

GOCHUJANG-GLAZED MUSHROOM & WHOLEGRAIN RICE BOWLS

300 g/1½ cups wholegrain brown rice, rinsed
2 tsp gochujang or sweet chilli sauce
2 tbsp rice wine or Amontillado sherry
2 tbsp light soy sauce
2 tsp sugar (just 1 tsp if using sweet chilli sauce)
1 tbsp vegetable oil
1 garlic clove, chopped
thumb-sized piece of fresh ginger, chopped into fine strips
2 spring onions/scallions, white parts only, cut into short lengths
½ red (bell) pepper, cut into strips
400 g/14 oz. assorted fresh oyster, shiitake, king oyster or shiroshimeji mushrooms, any large ones sliced
50 g/⅔ cup mangetout/snowpeas, cut into short pieces
2 tbsp raw cashew nuts
salt and freshly ground black pepper
handful of fresh coriander/cilantro sprigs, to garnish

SERVES 4

Place the rice in a heavy-based saucepan. Add 400 ml/1⅔ cups water and season with a pinch of salt. Bring to the boil, then reduce the heat, cover and simmer over a low heat for 25 minutes until the rice is tender.

About 5 minutes before the rice is ready, mix together the gochujang, rice wine, soy sauce and sugar in a small bowl to form a paste.

Heat the oil in a wok or large frying pan/skillet over a medium–high heat. Add the garlic, ginger and spring onions. Fry, stirring, for about 1 minute until fragrant. Add the red pepper, mushrooms, mangetout and cashews and stir-fry over a high heat for 2–3 minutes until the mushrooms are lightly browned. Add the gochujang paste mixture and stir in well to coat the ingredients. Stir-fry for 1–2 minutes until all the vegetables and mushrooms are glazed and sticky.

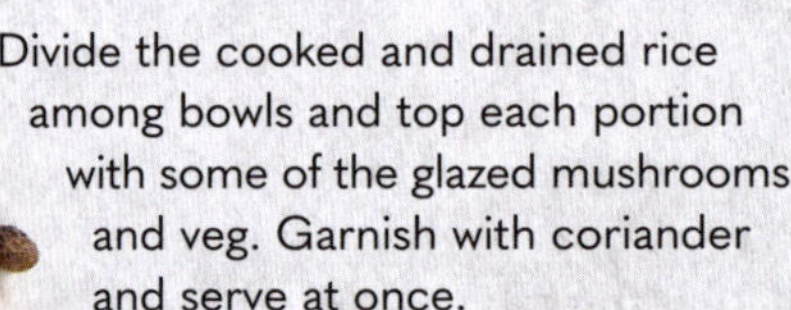

Divide the cooked and drained rice among bowls and top each portion with some of the glazed mushrooms and veg. Garnish with coriander and serve at once.

In all Asian dishes you will find a lovely balance of strong and delicate flavours. Here we have the richness of pork belly, the mellow flavour of noodles, the zing of pickled vegetables and finally a sweet, sour dressing.

BARBECUE PORK NOODLE BOWLS WITH DIPPING SAUCE

500 g/1 lb. 2 oz. pork belly strips, each cut into 3 pieces
3 tbsp fish sauce
2 tbsp ketjap manis
1 tsp Chinese five-spice powder
½ tsp freshly ground black pepper
4 garlic cloves, crushed
250 g/9 oz. dried rice stick noodles
125 g/2⅓ cups beansprouts, trimmed
8–12 cup-shaped leaves from an iceberg/butter lettuce
a selection of fresh herbs, such as mint, coriander/cilantro and Thai basil
pickled vegetables, to serve (optional)

a roasting pan lined with baking parchment

SERVES 4

Place the pork belly in a shallow dish. Whisk the fish sauce, ketjap manis, five-spice, pepper and garlic cloves together, and pour over the pork. Cover and set in the fridge to marinate overnight.

Preheat the oven to 180°C/160°C fan/350°F/gas 4.

Transfer the pork belly to the prepared roasting pan and roast in the preheated oven for 1 hour, turning halfway through, until the pork is golden, sticky and tender. Leave to cool for about 30 minutes until just warm and cut into pieces.

Meanwhile, put the noodles in a bowl, cover with boiling water and soak for 30 minutes until softened. Drain the noodles, pat dry and divide among serving bowls. Arrange the pork, beansprouts, lettuce leaves and herbs on plates around the table for people to help themselves. Serve with some pickled vegetables if liked.

Banh mi is the name for a Vietnamese barbecued pork and vegetable sub (baguette) served as street food. Here it is adapted into an equally delicious pork rice bowl with the signature sweet, sticky sauce.

BANH MI RICE BOWL

Place the pork belly strips in a bowl. Combine the pork marinade ingredients and pour over the pork strips, turning to coat thoroughly. Leave to marinate for 30 minutes.

Cook the rice according to the packet instructions and keep warm while you cook.

Heat the oil in a heavy-based frying pan/skillet over a high heat and fry the marinated pork strips, in batches, for about 2 minutes each side until charred. Cool for a few minutes, then slice thinly.

Divide the rice among bowls and arrange the pork and pickled vegetables on top along with the salad leaves and fresh herbs. Serve with sweet chilli sauce and crispy shallots.

600 g/1 lb. 5 oz. pork belly strips, skin removed
400 g/2¼ cups jasmine rice
2 tbsp vegetable oil

PORK MARINADE
2½ tbsp hoisin sauce
2 tbsp honey
4 tbsp light soy sauce
1 tbsp Shaoxing wine
½ tsp sesame oil
½ tsp Chinese five-spice

TO SERVE
pickled vegetables
handful of salad leaves
a few fresh coriander, mint and basil leaves
sweet chilli sauce
crispy shallots (see page 47)

SERVES 4

Tamarind is one of the ingredients used in Southeast Asia to impart the sour flavour for which the cuisine is renowned. Here, paired with the prawns/shrimp, asparagus and crab, it is quite delightful.

PRAWN, CRAB & TAMARIND RICE NOODLES

Soak the noodles in a bowlful of hot water for 10–20 minutes until softened. Drain well, shake dry and set aside in a large mixing bowl.

To make the sauce, whisk all the ingredients together in a small mixing bowl, stirring well to dissolve the sugar. Set aside.

Heat the oil in a wok or large frying pan/skillet set over a medium–high heat. Add the garlic, stir-fry for 10 seconds and then add the onion and pepper. Stir-fry for 2 minutes, then add the prawns and asparagus and continue to stir-fry for 2 minutes until the prawns are cooked through.

Add the crab meat and tamarind sauce and cook for 2 minutes. Add the noodles, spring onions and coriander, stir-fry until the noodles are heated through and serve immediately with extra coriander sprinkled on top.

NOTE *Tamarind can be bought whole in pods, as a block of hard pulp or as a concentrate. To make tamarind water, dilute the concentrate three parts to one part water and use as instructed.*

200 g/7 oz. glass (cellophane) noodles

2 tbsp peanut oil

4 garlic cloves, sliced

1 red onion, sliced

½ tbsp freshly ground black pepper

350 g/4¼ cups (about 35) raw prawns/shrimp, peeled, deveined and butterflied

350 g/3 cups asparagus tips, trimmed and cut into 5-cm/2-inch pieces

250 g/½ cup picked fresh crab meat

2 spring onions/scallions, sliced

4 tbsp chopped fresh coriander/ cilantro, plus extra to serve

TAMARIND SAUCE

125 ml/½ cup tamarind water (see Note left)

2 tbsp fish sauce

2 tbsp grated palm sugar/jaggery

SERVES 4

This is a surprisingly successful fusion of Hawaiian and Japanese cuisine and a take on a Japanese favourite, Nasu Denganku. The sticky aubergine/eggplant poke is so moreish.

STICKY AUBERGINE POKE WITH SOUR CARROT SALAD

900 g/2 lb. aubergines/ eggplants
4 shallots
125 g/$^{2}/_{3}$ cup demerara/ turbinado sugar
2 garlic cloves, crushed
1$^{1}/_{2}$ tsp crushed green peppercorns
75 ml/5 tbsp soy sauce
small handful of kale, chopped
250 g/1$^{1}/_{2}$ cups cooked sushi rice
small handful of coriander/ cilantro, chopped

SOUR CARROT SALAD

3 spring onions/scallions
200 g/1$^{1}/_{2}$ cups finely grated carrots
1 tbsp demerara/turbinado sugar
$^{1}/_{4}$ tsp salt
1 tbsp boiling water
freshly squeezed juice of 1 large lime
1 tsp rice wine vinegar

SERVES 4 AS AN APPETIZER

First make the carrot salad. Finely slice the spring onions diagonally into long strands. Mix the grated carrots and spring onions in a bowl. Dissolve the sugar and salt in the boiling water. Stir in the lime juice and vinegar and add this dressing to the carrot and onion mix. Set aside.

Cut the aubergines into 2.5-cm/1-inch cubes. Finely slice the shallots. Have them both at hand when you are making the caramel as you will have to act quickly.

Place the sugar in a large wok set over a high heat. Swirl the wok to help melt the sugar. The sugar will have a lovely amber tone. After about 5 minutes it will start to caramelize at the edges and you will notice a caramel smell. Swirl the wok once more to distribute the caramel evenly, then add the aubergines and shallots. Toss until the chunks are well coated, then cook for 2 minutes. Lower the heat, add the garlic and green peppercorns and cook for 2 minutes. Add the soy sauce and simmer, loosely covered with foil, for 7 minutes or until the sauce reduces to a thick consistency.

To serve, divide the carrot salad, aubergine mixture, kale and rice between four bowls. Scatter over the coriander.

NOTE *To make this more Japanese, add a teaspoon of white miso paste before you add the soy sauce.*

The crispier the better for these pork pieces. It's best to make the pieces really dark and crunchy, and adding the lime towards the end of frying is a great way to crisp them up and perfect the balance with the sweetness.

SWEET CHILLI PORK BELLY & NOODLES

A few hours in advance, or the day before, marinate the pork belly to really give it flavour. Put the diced, rindless belly pieces in a bag or bowl with the chilli, honey, paprika, garlic and sesame oil. Seal and leave in the fridge for a few hours or overnight.

Heat the vegetable oil in a wok or high-sided frying pan/skillet and fry the spring onions, red pepper and pak choi over a high heat until they are soft and starting to brown. Transfer them to a plate and set aside.

Spoon the belly pieces out of the marinade (keep the marinade) and coat them in the flour. Add to the wok and fry over a high heat until they become crisp (and smell amazing!), then add the marinade and fry for 4–5 minutes until the pork is cooked through.

Squeeze in the lime juice to help them crisp some more. Return the cooked vegetables to the wok along with a pinch of salt and pepper. Stir well, then serve with noodles and soy sauce. Sprinkle some more chopped red chilli on the top to add an extra fresh kick, if you like.

400 g/14 oz. rindless pork belly, diced

1 red chilli/chile, deseeded and finely chopped, plus extra to serve (optional)

2 tbsp clear honey

2 tsp ground paprika

1 garlic clove, finely chopped

1 tbsp sesame oil

1 tbsp vegetable oil

8–10 spring onions/scallions, trimmed and finely sliced

1 red (bell) pepper, deseeded and finely chopped

2 pak choi/bok choy, trimmed and chopped

1 tbsp plain/all-purpose flour

freshly squeezed juice of 1 lime

pinch each of salt and black pepper

TO SERVE

1 lime, cut into wedges

cooked noodles

soy sauce

SERVES 2

This dish combines two delicious dishes that are just too hard to choose between in a Chinese restaurant!

SWEET & SOUR ORANGE CHICKEN WITH PINEAPPLE FRIED RICE

675 g/1½ lbs. boneless skinless chicken, chopped into bite-sized pieces

2 eggs

1 tsp salt

ground white pepper, to taste

1 litre/quart groundnut/peanut oil, for frying

40 g/⅓ cup cornflour/cornstarch, plus 1 tbsp for thickening

35 g/¼ cup plain/all-purpose flour

4 rings fresh (or canned) pineapple, drained (juice reserved)

1 tbsp fresh ginger, peeled and grated

1 tsp garlic, minced

2 green (bell) peppers, in small pieces

½ tbsp chilli flakes/hot red pepper flakes

2 spring onions/scallions, thinly sliced on a diagonal

1 tbsp rice wine

store-bought sweet & sour sauce, to serve

PINEAPPLE FRIED RICE

8 rings fresh (or canned) pineapple, drained

2 tbsp canola oil

1 tsp garlic, minced

1 tsp fresh ginger, peeled and grated

½ onion, chopped

1 red (bell) pepper, chopped

½ carrot, grated

240 g/2 cups cooked rice

1–2 tbsp light soy sauce

1 tsp Madras curry powder

caster/granulated sugar, to taste

1 spring onion/scallion, thinly sliced on a diagonal

SERVES 4

Place the chicken pieces in a large bowl. Be sure to handle raw chicken with care. In another large bowl, stir together the eggs, salt, pepper and 1 tablespoon of the oil. Mix well. In a small bowl, whisk the 40 g/⅓ cup cornflour and flour together. Mix the flour mixture into egg mixture. Add the chicken pieces, tossing to coat.

Heat the rest of the oil in a large frying pan/skillet, wok or deep-fryer to 190°C/375°F or until the oil is bubbling steadily. Add the chicken pieces, a few at a time. Fry for 3–4 minutes or until golden crisp.

Remove the chicken from the oil with a slotted spoon; drain on paper towels then set aside. Clean the wok or frying pan/skillet and heat for 15 seconds over a high heat. Add a little oil and then add the ginger and garlic. Stir-fry for 10 seconds or until fragrant. Add the peppers, chilli flakes, spring onions, and rice wine. Stir for a few seconds. Add the sweet and sour sauce and bring to the boil. Add the cooked chicken, stirring until well mixed.

Stir 60 ml/1 cup water into the extra 1 tablespoon cornflour until smooth and add to the chicken. Heat until the sauce has thickened and then turn off the gas.

To make the pineapple rice, cut the pineapple rings into small wedges. Heat a wok or frying pan over a medium heat. Add the oil. Once hot, add the garlic and ginger. Stir-fry for 30 seconds. Add the onion. Stir-fry for 1 minute, then add the red pepper, grated carrot and pineapple. Mix everything together and then add the cooked rice and fry for 2 minutes. Stir the mixture and toss in the pan until it looks shiny. Add the soy sauce and stir in. Stir in the curry powder and sugar. Stir in the spring onion or use as a garnish.

MAIN PLATES & SHARERS

Sweet & Spicy Glazed Ham

Pulled Pork Shoulder

Crispy Chilli Beef

Shoyu Chicken

Maple & Ginger Turkey Crown

Miso Butterfish

Sesame Ginger Fish

Soy & Sesame Baked Monkfish & Greens in a Caramelized Tamari Butter Dressing

Salmon Inferno with Karedok Salad

Sticky Plum-roasted Cabbages

Miso & Umeboshi Baked Pumpkin

Sticky Sesame Aubergine with Gochujang Ketchup

A very simple way of feeding a lot of people, this gives a little chilli twist to a classic baked ham and is perfect for any time of year.

SWEET & SPICY GLAZED HAM

3–4 sprigs of fresh thyme
2 fresh bay leaves
sprig of fresh parsley
4.5-kg/10-lb. ham on the bone
1 carrot, roughly chopped
1 onion, roughly chopped
2 celery sticks/ribs, roughly chopped
7–8 black peppercorns
3 whole cloves
330-ml/12-oz. can or bottle of stout beer (e.g. Guinness or Mackeson)
3 tbsp sweet chilli sauce
2 tbsp pure maple syrup
2 tbsp Dijon mustard

SERVES 12–14

Tie the thyme, bay leaves and parsley together with kitchen twine to make a bouquet garni.

Place the ham in a heatproof casserole dish, add the bouquet garni, carrot, onion, celery, peppercorns, cloves and beer. Top up with cold water until the ham is covered. Set over a medium heat and bring to the boil. Reduce the heat, partially cover with the lid and gently simmer for about 3 hours. If it starts to look dry, add only boiling water.

At the end of cooking, remove the dish from the heat and set aside for 20–30 minutes to cool with the ham still in the cooking stock.

Preheat the oven to 200°C/180°C fan/400°F/gas 6.

Remove the ham from the dish and place on a large board. Cut away and discard the skin, leaving an even layer of fat exposed all over the meat. Place the ham in a large roasting pan and, with a sharp knife, score the fat in a diamond pattern, making sure not to cut through to the meat.

Mix the sweet chilli sauce, maple syrup and mustard thoroughly with a balloon whisk. Spread this glaze evenly over the ham, ensuring it is well coated. Roast the ham in the preheated oven for about 30–40 minutes until nicely browned and the glaze has formed a golden crust. Baste the meat with the glaze that runs into the roasting pan during cooking.

Let the ham rest for a few minutes before carving, then serve hot with your choice of sides or cold.

NOTE *This recipe requires a good-quality sweet chilli sauce, ideally one containing a little ginger, garlic and lime juice as this will add a delicious depth of flavour as well as the gentle chilli warmth.*

You can't beat succulent, melt-in-the-mouth pulled pork for a satisfying meal. Combine it with an unctuous, sweet and sticky barbecue sauce and you'll have a real crowd pleaser.

PULLED PORK SHOULDER

3 kg/6½ lb. free-range, bone-in pork shoulder (rind on, if you would like to make crackling)
1 tbsp sea salt (flakes or crystals)
3 tbsp olive oil
1 tsp paprika
big pinch of cayenne pepper
warm brioche rolls, to serve

BARBECUE SAUCE

1 tbsp olive oil
1 white onion, chopped
1 garlic clove, chopped
2 red (bell) peppers, deseeded and chopped
pinch of fennel seeds
pinch of cumin
½ tsp mustard powder
½ tsp salt
1 tbsp soft brown sugar
pinch of black pepper
400 g/14 oz. canned tomatoes, drained
1 cooking apple, cored, peeled and diced
100 ml/generous ⅓ cup cider vinegar
3½ tbsp maple syrup
100 ml/generous ⅓ cup apple juice
½ tsp Dijon mustard

SERVES 10–12

Preheat the oven to 190°C/170°C fan/375°F/gas 5.

If you want to make crackling, use a sharp knife to score diagonal lines across the rind and push the salt into the cuts in the rind. This draws the moisture out of the rind and fat so that the surface crackles.

Fold a large piece of foil in two to make it double-strength and place it in a roasting pan. You're going to need enough foil either side to cover and seal the pork. Place the pork on top. Drizzle the olive oil over the surface and sprinkle over the paprika and cayenne.

Keeping the foil open at this stage, place the meat in the oven and roast for 25 minutes so that the outside has a chance to brown. Turn the temperature right down to 150°C/130°C fan/300°F/gas 2, fold in the sides of the foil so that the meat is totally covered and cook for at least 3 hours, or 4 hours if you can. Every hour, open up the foil and baste the meat by spooning the juices from the bottom of the pan back over the top of the joint. After 3–4 hours, prod it with a fork and see if it is easy to 'pull' (the strips in the muscle should have 'melted' apart). Return for a little longer if it still feels tight.

Meanwhile, make the barbecue sauce. Heat the oil in a pan over a medium heat and sauté the onion, garlic and red pepper for about 4–5 minutes until softened. Stir in the fennel seeds, cumin, mustard powder, salt, sugar and pepper. Add the remaining ingredients and bring to the boil, then turn the heat down to a simmer and cook for 1 hour, stirring occasionally. If it's looking very thick, add a drop more apple juice. Remove from the heat and allow to cool a little, then whizz in a food processor until smooth.

Open the foil on the pork, increase the heat to 200°C/180°C fan/400°F/gas 6 and continue to cook for 5 minutes to crisp up the top. Remove the crackling and set aside. Use two forks to 'pull' the pork to shreds. Use scissors to cut the crackling into thin strips. Serve the pork in warm brioche rolls with barbecue sauce and crackling on the side.

This recipe is reminiscent of that all-time favourite Chinese takeaway dish. This one has a slightly cleaner feel, but is still irresistibly sweet and sticky.

CRISPY CHILLI BEEF

600 g/21 oz. rump steak
1 tsp Chinese five spice
300 g/3 cups cornflour/ cornstarch
2 eggs
250 ml/1 cup vegetable oil, for frying
5-cm/2-inch piece of fresh ginger, chopped
3 garlic cloves, chopped
1 fresh red jalapeño chilli/ chile, finely diced, plus extra slices to garnish
6 spring onions/scallions, cut into 5-cm/2-inch lengths
snipped chives, to garnish
cooked basmati rice, to serve

SAUCE

45 ml/3 tbsp cider vinegar
45 ml/3 tbsp runny honey
60 ml/¼ cup tomato ketchup
45 ml/3 tbsp sweet chilli/ chili sauce
15 ml/1 tbsp dark soy sauce
a pinch of salt

SERVES 4

Put all the ingredients for the sauce in a bowl, add 60 ml/¼ cup water and mix to combine. Set aside.

Place cling film/plastic wrap over the steaks and lightly bash them with a rolling pin (or base of a saucepan) – this tenderizes the meat and will also make for much thinner strips. Pop the steaks in the freezer for 15 minutes to firm up slightly and make them easier to slice thinly.

Slice the steaks against the grain (widthways) into thin strips, 3 mm/⅛ inch thick and lightly dust in the Chinese five spice.

Place the cornflour in a mixing bowl. Break the eggs into a separate bowl and beat them.

Drop the steak strips into the cornflour to coat, then shake off any excess flour and dip into beaten egg. Shake off any excess and place them back in the cornflour (they will clump together but keep shaking them about and they will separate).

Heat the oil in a large, heavy-based saucepan until shimmering. Carefully fry the steak strips for 3 minutes, or until crisp (you might need to do this in batches). Remove from the oil using a slotted spoon and place on a plate lined with paper towels. Set the pan aside but don't discard the oil. Once all the steak strips have been fried and left to cool for 5 minutes, reheat the oil and, once shimmering, fry the steak strips for a second time for 1 minute – this double-fry creates extra crispy strips! Transfer to a plate lined with clean paper towels.

Heat a splash of oil in a clean frying pan/skillet set over a high heat. Sauté the ginger, garlic, chilli and spring onions for a minute – don't let them burn. Pour in the sauce; it will start bubbling immediately. After 30 seconds, or just as the sauce starts to thicken, throw in the crispy beef strips and stir just to coat them in the sauce, then remove from the pan straight away and put into a serving dish. Garnish with snipped chives and some slices of red chilli and serve with plenty of basmati rice.

This is almost every Hawaiian's favourite dish and is so easy to make. The salty savouriness of the soy sauce with the chicken makes this a warm, comforting dish. Traditionally, locals use chicken thighs with the skin on and bone in, but boneless, skinless chicken thighs or breast works just as well.

SHOYU CHICKEN

450 g/1 lb. boneless, skinless chicken breasts
450 g/1 lb. boneless, skinless chicken thighs
235 ml/1 cup soy sauce
200 g/1 cup brown sugar
1 tbsp apple cider vinegar
1 tbsp Worcestershire sauce
1 heaped tbsp finely chopped fresh ginger
1 heaped tbsp finely chopped garlic
sticky white rice, to serve
your favourite pickles, sliced spring onions/scallions, or sesame seeds, to garnish (optional)

SERVES 6

Combine all the ingredients, apart from the garnishes, in a storage container or ziplock bag with 235 ml/1 cup water. Marinate overnight in the refrigerator or for a minimum of 8 hours.

Tip the ingredients into a large, heavy-based stew pot and bring to the boil over a high heat, stirring occasionally to ensure nothing sticks to the bottom of the pot. Once boiling, reduce the heat to low, cover and simmer for 30 minutes or until the chicken is tender and cooked through. Stir occasionally and skim the fat off the top as necessary.

Using a slotted spoon, remove the chicken from the pot and place on a chopping board or serving platter. Loosely cover with foil to keep warm.

Bring the sauce back to the boil, reduce the heat and simmer for about 10 minutes. Remove from the heat and let the sauce cool and thicken slightly for 10 minutes.

Serve with sticky white rice and drizzle the remaining sauce over the rice and chicken. Garnish with pickles, sliced spring onions or sesame seeds.

NOTE *For a thicker gravy, add 3 tablespoons cornflour/cornstarch mixed with a little water after you remove the chicken from the pot. Or, after removing the chicken from the pot and while the sauce is reducing, shred the chicken meat, then add it back into the reduced sauce. Serve immediately.*

MAPLE & GINGER TURKEY CROWN
WITH SWEET POTATOES & DEVILS ON HORSEBACK

Preheat the oven to 190°C/170°C fan/375°F/gas 5.

Put the turkey crown into a large roasting pan with plenty of space around the sides. Drizzle with olive oil and season with salt and pepper. Cover the turkey with foil and put into the preheated oven to roast for 20 minutes per kilogram or 12 minutes per pound, plus 1 hour 10 minutes. Halfway through cooking, add the sweet potatoes, garlic, onions, bay leaves and rosemary to the pan and season. Return to the oven to finish cooking while you make the glaze.

Put the shallots, ginger, garlic and olive oil in a small, heavy saucepan and cook over a low heat for about 5–7 minutes, stirring occasionally, until softened. Add the remaining ingredients, then bring to the boil and cook, stirring, for 3–5 minutes. Reduce the heat to medium and simmer for 10 minutes until thickened. Strain out the onion, ginger and garlic and finely mince using a sharp knife, then stir back into the glaze. Remove from the heat and leave to cool to room temperature. Cover and refrigerate the glaze until needed.

When the turkey has 20 minutes left, carefully remove from the oven, remove the foil and brush with the maple and ginger glaze. Add the devils on horseback to the pan now, if using. Return the turkey to the oven (uncovered) for the remaining 20 minutes.

Check that the turkey is cooked through by piercing the thickest part with a knife – the juices should run clear. Transfer the cooked turkey to a warm serving plate but keep the veggies and devils on horseback warm in a low oven. Cover the turkey with foil and rest for at least 10 minutes before carving and serving.

2.3 kg/4½ lb. turkey crown
1 tsp olive oil
4 sweet potatoes, peeled and cut into wedges
1 whole head garlic, sliced in half widthways
3 red onions, peeled and cut into wedges
4 bay leaves
3 sprigs fresh rosemary
sea salt and freshly ground black pepper

MAPLE & GINGER GLAZE

2 banana shallots, peeled and finely chopped
1 x 5-cm/2-inch thumb of ginger, peeled and grated
4 garlic cloves, peeled and crushed
2 tbsp olive oil
grated zest and freshly squeezed juice of 1 orange
2 tbsp kecap manis (Indonesian sweet soy sauce)
2 tbsp soy sauce
4 tbsp maple syrup

SERVES 6–8

DEVILS ON HORSEBACK

Season the pecans with sea salt and drizzle with oil, then stuff one inside each prune where the pit would have been (using a knife to make a larger incision if needed) with a shaving of Parmesan.

Wrap each stuffed prune in a piece of pancetta and set aside until ready to cook with the turkey. Alternatively, bake separately in an oven preheated to 190°C/170°C fan/375°F/gas 5 for 20 minutes.

12 pecan nuts
extra virgin olive oil, for drizzling
12 prunes, pitted
12 Parmesan shavings
6 pancetta slices, halved widthways
sea salt

This recipe is perfect for an easy Thanksgiving or celebration meal. It would go well with classic green vegetables or a simple crunchy slaw.

This recipe is a great option for entertaining as, apart from being utterly delicious and guaranteed to impress, you can prep it in advance. Try serving it with some pickled ginger if you have it.

MISO BUTTERFISH

4 x 200-g/7-oz. black cod fillets, or sablefish (Chilean sea bass and salmon also work well)
235 ml/1 cup sake
235 ml/1 cup mirin
250 g/1 cup white miso paste
150 g/¾ cup granulated sugar
1 tbsp furikake seasoning
25 g/⅓ cup spring onions/scallions, finely sliced (optional)

SERVES 4

Rinse the fish. Gently but thoroughly pat dry with paper towels. Set aside.

Place the sake and mirin in a heavy-based pan and bring to the boil over a high heat. Boil for a few minutes to cook off the alcohol, then simmer for 10 minutes.

Whisk in the miso paste until fully dissolved. Add the sugar, stirring continuously to make sure it doesn't stick to the bottom of the pan and burn. Simmer over a low heat for about 45 minutes, stirring occasionally. The marinade will thicken slightly and caramelize. Cool to room temperature.

Once the marinade has cooled completely, put three-quarters into a non-metallic, sealable storage container or ziplock bag. Add the fish, ensuring it is completely coated. Refrigerate for 2–3 days, stirring occasionally to ensure the fish is well marinated. Reserve the remaining marinade in the fridge to use later.

Preheat the oven to 180°C/160°C fan/350°F/gas 4.

Remove the fish from the marinade, but leave a good coating on the fish. Lay the fish on a baking sheet and bake in the preheated oven for about 10 minutes.

Preheat the grill/broiler to medium-high. Pour a little of the reserved marinade over each baked fish fillet and grill/broil for 3–5 minutes, or until golden brown and caramelized.

Drizzle any remaining marinade over the fish, sprinkle with furikake, and top with sliced spring onions. Serve immediately with steamed greens and rice.

NOTE *You can also use this marinade recipe with chicken, just cook it for a little longer in the oven, ensuring the meat is cooked through before you put it under the grill/broiler.*

An easy recipe where the sauce is the star of the show. The sesame mixed with the sweetness of the honey and the saltiness of the shoyu is one of those really moreish combinations. Make extra to mix with mayonnaise for an island-style version of tartare sauce. It also works nicely with things like chicken, aubergine/eggplant or prawns/shrimp.

SESAME GINGER FISH

450 g/1 lb. fish fillets, such as salmon or halibut, deboned
vegetable oil, for greasing
1 bunch spring onions/scallions, finely sliced, to garnish (green bits only)
1 tsp toasted sesame seeds, to garnish

SAUCE
1 tbsp finely chopped fresh ginger
1 tbsp sesame seeds
2 tbsp honey
2 tbsp shoyu
freshly ground black pepper

TO SERVE
your favourite pickles (pickled ginger works well)
steamed green vegetables
steamed white rice

SERVES 4

Mix together all the sauce ingredients in a small bowl. Brush generously over the fish.

Brush a grill/broiler pan, non-stick griddle pan or barbecue with vegetable oil.

Grill or sear the fish fillets over a medium-high heat for a few minutes on each side, depending on the type of fish, size of the fillets and how well you like your fish cooked.

Garnish with spring onions and the toasted sesame seeds. Serve immediately with your favourite pickles, steamed green vegetables and steamed white rice.

This sticky caramelized tamari butter works beautifully with the meaty monkfish for a stylish yet fuss-free meal.

SOY & SESAME BAKED MONKFISH
& GREENS IN A CARAMELIZED TAMARI BUTTER DRESSING

Preheat the oven to 180°C/160°C fan/350°F/gas 4.

Lay the monkfish tail on the prepared baking sheet. Fill the cut where the bone used to be with the ginger, lime wedges, spring onions and garlic. Tie the fish up securely with the cooking string in rounds spaced evenly widthways along the length of the fish.

In a bowl, mix together all the ingredients for the marinade. Drizzle the marinade over the fish and bake in the oven for 25–30 minutes or until cooked through, basting with the cooking juices halfway through cooking.

Meanwhile, for the seaweed crumb, mix together the ground wasabi peas, seaweed and black sesame seeds and set aside.

Sprinkle the baked fish with the seaweed crumb just before serving with the noodles, spring onions, pickled ginger, daikon radishes, lime wedges and the greens in their tamari butter dressing (see overleaf).

Continued on page 130

1 x 1.5-kg/3 lb. 5-oz. monkfish tail fillet (skin and bone removed – you can ask your fishmonger to do this)

thumb-sized piece of fresh ginger, peeled and julienned

1 lime, cut into thin wedges

2 spring onions/scallions, halved lengthways

2 garlic cloves, thinly sliced

MARINADE

4 tbsp soy sauce

2 tbsp sesame oil

1 tbsp runny honey

1 garlic clove, finely chopped

thumb-sized piece of fresh ginger, peeled and finely grated

grated zest and freshly squeezed juice of 1 lime

1 tbsp black sesame seeds

SEAWEED CRUMB

2 tbsp wasabi peas, coarsely blitzed in a food processor

1 tbsp dried seaweed, crumbled

1 tbsp black sesame seeds

TO SERVE

200 g/7 oz. cooked soba (buckwheat) noodles

thinly sliced spring onions/scallions

pickled ginger

sliced daikon radishes

lime wedges

baking sheet, lined with baking parchment

cooking string

SERVES 4

GREENS IN CARAMELIZED TAMARI BUTTER DRESSING

Melt the butter in a frying pan/skillet over a medium heat. As the butter melts, it will begin to foam. The colour will progress from yellow to golden to, finally, a toasty-brown. As soon as you see the colour change and smell that nutty aroma, add the tamari or soy sauce and chilli, then turn the heat to low and cook for 1 minute.

Finally, stir in the garlic and keep warm while you cook the vegetables. Cook the broccoli in a large saucepan of boiling water for 2 minutes. Add the baby pak choi to the same pan and cook for 1 minute more. Drain the vegetables well.

Dress the vegetables in the caramelized tamari butter and serve alongside the baked monkfish.

50 g/3½ tbsp butter
2 tbsp tamari or soy sauce
1 red chilli/chile, finely chopped
2 garlic cloves, crushed
200 g/7 oz. Tenderstem broccoli
4 baby pak choi/ bok choy

Here, hot and spicy Asian salmon is paired with a fresh and fragrant Indonesian-style salad. Saltiness and crunch are provided by a peanut dressing and prawn/shrimp crackers served on the side. This dish can work well as a shared appetizer or light lunch, but it is also perfect for a quick evening meal during the week.

SALMON INFERNO WITH KAREDOK SALAD

600-g/1 lb. 5-oz. salmon fillet
1 tbsp olive oil
2 garlic cloves, finely grated
2 tbsp fish sauce
freshly squeezed juice of 2 limes
2 tbsp sambal oelek (or other hot chilli/chile paste)
1–3 tbsp palm sugar/jaggery
1 tbsp peanut/groundnut oil

TO SERVE
lime wedges
Karedok Salad (see page 133)
fresh Thai basil, mint and coriander/cilantro
prawn/shrimp crackers
sweet chilli/chile sauce

large roasting pan, lined with baking parchment or foil

SERVES 4

Preheat the oven to 200°C/180°C fan/400°F/gas 6.

Brush the salmon skin with the oil and place it, skin-side down, in the prepared roasting pan.

In a bowl, mix together the garlic, fish sauce, lime juice, sambal oelek, palm sugar and peanut oil. Spread this mixture evenly over the salmon flesh.

Roast in the preheated oven for about 20 minutes or until the salmon is cooked through – check by poking a knife into the thickest part of the fillet and making sure the fish flakes easily.

Serve directly from the pan or use a couple of fish slices to carefully lift the salmon onto a serving platter. Serve the fish with lime wedges for squeezing over, Karedok Salad (see overleaf), fresh herbs, prawn crackers and sweet chilli sauce.

Illustrated on page 133

KAREDOK SALAD

Gently toss all the ingredients for the salad together and serve on the serving platter or in the pan with the salmon.

In a food processor, pulse together all the ingredients for the dressing until coarsely blitzed, and serve drizzled over the salad.

200 g/7 oz. fine green/French beans, cooked and cut into 3-cm/1-inch lengths

1 small Chinese cabbage, thinly sliced (on a mandoline if you have one)

1 large cucumber, cut into julienne

100 g/1¾ cups beansprouts

handful fresh Thai basil

4 shallots, thinly sliced into rounds

DRESSING

2–3 tbsp peanut/groundnut oil

150 g/1¼ cups unsalted peanuts, toasted

1 tsp galangal paste

1–2 red chillies/chiles, chopped

2 garlic cloves, roughly chopped

freshly squeezed juice of 2–3 limes

2 tbsp palm sugar/jaggery

2 tbsp light soy sauce

½ tsp shrimp paste

Deliciously sticky and juicy – who would have thought that cabbages could taste this good? Perfect served with glazed cashews, green beans and crunchy tofu chips.

STICKY PLUM-ROASTED CABBAGES
WITH GREEN BEANS & GLAZED CASHEWS & TOFU CHIPS

Preheat the oven to 180°C/160°C fan/350°F/gas 4.

Combine all the plum sauce ingredients in a small saucepan over a low-medium heat, stirring occasionally, for about 10–15 minutes until the sugar and spices have dissolved and you have a smooth sauce.

Arrange the cabbage slices, plums and red onion on the prepared baking pans and drizzle evenly with the oil and then the sauce, reserving a little sauce to serve on the side of the dish. Roast in the preheated oven for 25–30 minutes. The cabbages should be browned and sticky but still have some bite when cooked.

Serve with the reserved plum sauce on the side, the Tofu Chips and Green Beans and Glazed Cashews (see overleaf).

Continued on page 136

½ green cabbage, cut into thick slices
½ red cabbage, cut into thick slices
5 plums, pitted and cut into wedges
2 red onions, cut into wedges
2 tbsp flavourless oil

PLUM SAUCE

thumb-sized piece of fresh ginger, peeled and finely grated
150 g/¾ cup soft light brown sugar
150 ml/⅔ cup apple cider vinegar
1 tbsp freshly squeezed lemon juice
1 tsp sea salt
1 tsp Chinese five-spice powder
½ tsp chilli flakes/hot red pepper flakes

2 baking pans, lined with baking parchment or foil

SERVES 4

TOFU CHIPS

2 x blocks 200 g/7 oz. firm tofu, drained and excess water pressed out
cooking oil spray
2 tsp sea salt
1 tsp onion powder
1 tbsp Sichuan pepper
pinch of cayenne pepper
½ tsp chilli/chili powder
baking sheet, lined with baking parchment

Preheat the oven to 150°C/130°C fan/300°F/gas 2.

Slice the tofu into very thin pieces, no more than 3-mm/⅛-inch-thick. Lay out the slices on the prepared baking sheet. Lightly mist the slices with a little cooking spray.

Bake in the preheated oven for about 25 minutes or until golden brown and crisp.

Mix together the remaining ingredients in a small bowl and sprinkle on the tofu chips to taste, then serve.

GREEN BEANS & GLAZED CASHEWS

300 g/10½ oz. green/French beans, trimmed
150 g/generous 1 cup raw cashews
1 tbsp soy sauce
4 tbsp rice vinegar
1 garlic clove, crushed
thumb-sized piece of fresh ginger, peeled and grated
1 tsp toasted sesame oil
1 tsp white sugar
sea salt

Bring a large pan of salted water to the boil. Add the green beans and bring back to the boil, then simmer for 3–5 minutes until just tender. Drain and plunge straight into a bowl of ice-cold water to stop the cooking process. Drain the beans well and dry with paper towels. Set aside.

Dry-toast the cashews in a small frying pan/skillet over a medium heat, shaking the pan to make sure they don't burn. Once toasted, turn the heat up to medium-high and add the soy sauce. Toss to coat and cook for about 30 seconds until the liquid has evaporated. Leave to cool completely.

In a large bowl, whisk together the rice vinegar, garlic, ginger, sesame oil and sugar. Add the green beans to the dressing and stir to coat. Serve topped with the soy-glazed cashews.

A vegetable-centric dish worthy of the main event! This delicous roasted pumpkin is perfect on a courgette/zucchini pancake with kimchi and a spoonful of Japanese mayonnaise.

MISO & UMEBOSHI BAKED PUMPKIN
WITH COURGETTE PANCAKES & QUICK KIMCHI

1 kabocha pumpkin or 3 small pumpkins
bunch of spring onions/ scallions
4 tbsp flavourless oil
2 tsp sesame oil
4 tbsp white miso paste
2 tbsp soy sauce
4 tbsp mirin
4 tsp umeboshi paste
cooking string (optional)
roasting pan, lined with baking parchment

SERVES 4–5

Preheat the oven to 180°C/160°C fan/350°F/gas 4.

Cut the pumpkin(s) in half lengthways and deseed. Cut the pumpkin(s) into 5 cm/2-inch thick wedges and tie loosely together with cooking string. Nestle the spring onions/scallions between the wedges and place in the prepared roasting pan. (Alternatively, you can spread the wedges and onions in a roasting pan without tying.)

Mix together the remaining ingredients in a small bowl with 2 tablespoons water to make a marinade and brush generously all over the pumpkin slices.

Roast in the preheated oven for 30–40 minutes for 1 medium pumpkin (or 30–35 for 3 smaller) turning over halfway through until tender. Shake the pan to coat the pumpkin pieces in the sticky marinade and remove to a serving plate. Serve with the courgette pancakes and quick kimchi (see overleaf).

Continued on page 139

COURGETTE PANCAKES

Put the flour and a big pinch of salt in a bowl and whisk in the eggs. Whisk in 200–250 ml/¾–1 cup plus 1 tablespoon water (as needed) to make a thick batter. Leave to rest at room temperature for 10 minutes.

Add the grated courgettes, the oil, spring onions, Chinese five-spice (if using) and some black pepper to the batter and mix thoroughly.

Heat a little oil in a large frying pan/skillet and, when it's very hot, ladle in enough mixture to cover the base of the pan completely. Cook over a medium heat for 2–3 minutes until the underneath is set, then slide it out onto a plate and invert it back into the pan to cook the other side. Keep the cooked pancakes warm in a low oven while you use up the batter. Using a large frying pan, you should get 4 thick pancakes.

250 g/1¾ cups plus 2 tbsp plain/all-purpose flour
2 eggs
500 g/18 oz. green and yellow courgettes/zucchini, coarsely grated, salted and moisture squeezed out
1 tbsp flavourless oil, plus extra for frying
3 spring onions/scallions, finely chopped
½ tsp Chinese five-spice powder (optional)
sea salt and freshly ground black pepper

QUICK ASPARAGUS & CARROT KIMCHI

In a large bowl, toss together the sliced asparagus, carrots, salt and sugar.

Add the spring onions gochugaru paste (or crushed chilli flakes), garlic, fish sauce and ginger and toss well to coat.

Serve immediately or cover with cling film/plastic wrap and leave at room temperature for 2 days to allow fermentation to begin before refrigerating. This kimchi will keep for only a few days in the fridge as it is a quick version.

200 g/7 oz. asparagus, shaved into ribbons
200 g/7 oz. carrots, peeled and shaved into ribbons
1 tbsp sea salt
1 tbsp sugar
5 spring onions/scallions, cut into 5-cm/2-inch lengths
1 tbsp gochugaru paste (coarse Korean red chilli/chili pepper powder) or 1 tbsp chilli flakes/hot red pepper flakes, finely ground
2 garlic cloves, crushed
1 tbsp fish sauce
thumb-sized piece of fresh ginger, peeled and grated

Spoon into warm pitta bread, with crisp shredded lettuce and gochujang ketchup for the perfect sweet and sticky treat.

STICKY SESAME AUBERGINE WITH GOCHUJANG KETCHUP

Preheat the oven to 190°C/170°C fan/375°F/gas 5.

Cut the aubergines into bite-sized cubes and transfer them to a large bowl.

In a separate bowl, mix the sesame oil, olive oil, grated ginger, ketjap manis, soy sauce, 4 teaspoons gochujang paste, sugar and garlic. Stir everything together and pour the mixture over the aubergine cubes. Toss to coat everything well.

Spoon the aubergine evenly over a large, flat sheet pan and roast for about 25–30 minutes, until the aubergine is cooked. Scatter over the sesame seeds and chopped spring onions.

To make the gochujang ketchup, simply mix the gochujang paste with the tomato ketchup in a small bowl.

Scoop the aubergine mixture into warmed pitta breads, and add shredded lettuce and gochujang ketchup, as desired.

2 medium aubergines/ eggplants
2 tbsp sesame oil
2 tbsp olive oil
4-cm/1½-in. piece of fresh ginger, peeled and grated
4 tbsp ketjap manis (thick, sweet Indonesian soy sauce)
120 ml/½ cup dark soy sauce
4 tsp gochujang paste
2 tsp caster/granulated sugar
3 garlic cloves, minced
2–3 tbsp sesame seeds
bunch of spring onions/scallions, thinly sliced on a diagonal

GOCHUJANG KETCHUP
4 tbsp gochujang paste
4 tbsp good-quality tomato ketchup

TO SERVE
4 pitta breads, warmed
shredded lettuce

SERVES 4

INDEX

CREDITS

RECIPE CREDITS

Valerie Aikman-Smith
Korean Sticky Ribs

Miranda Ballard
Pulled Pork Shoulder
Sweet Chilli Pork Belly & Noodles

Ghillie Basan
Duck Satay with Grilled Pineapple & Plum Sauce

Jordan Bourke
Charred Shrimp with Nam Jim

James Campbell
Hirata Steamed Pork Buns

Maxine Clark
Kimchi & Meatball Pizza with Soy-Lime Glaze

Jess & Jo Edun
Guinness Pork Ribs
Mighty Supermalt Wings

Liz Franklin
Sticky Sesame Aubergine with Gochujang Ketchup

Carol Hilker
Chicago-Style Baby Back Ribs
Extra-Crunchy Crumbed Wings
Harissa-Honey Hot Wings
Honey-Srirarcha Wings
Kung Pao Wings
Maple Cured Bacon & Tomato Sandwich
Sake Wings
Sticky Asian Caramel Wings
Sticky Teriyaki Wings
Sweet & Sour Orange Chicken with Pineapple Fried Rice
Sweet & Spicy Wings

Atsuko Ikeda
Chicken Teriyaki with Lime on Quinoa Rice
Grilled Chicken Skewers
Miso & Maple marinated Salmon
Miso-Glazed Aubergine
Savoury Pancakes with Toppings
Spicy Tuna Tartare on Nori Chips

Jackie Kearney
Sweet & Sour Popcorn Tofu

Kathy Kordalis
Maple & Ginger Turkey Crown with Sweet Potatoes & Devils on Horseback
Miso & Umeboshi Baked Pumpkin with Courgette Pancakes & Quick Kimchi
Salmon Inferno with Karedok Salad
Soy & Sesame Baked Monkfish & Greens in a Caramelised Tamari Butter Dressing
Sticky Plum-Roasted Cabbages with Green Beans & Glazed Cashews & Tofu Chips
Sticky Rum Ribs

Jenny Linford
Tomato Ginger Spare Ribs

Loretta Liu
Beef Bulgogi & Rice Noodle Wraps
Hoisin Duck Puffs
Barbecue Pork Bao
Barbecue Pork Puffs

Uyen Luu
Vietnamese Barbecue Spareribs

Dan May
Sweet & Spicy Glazed Ham

Theo A. Michaels
Crispy Chilli Beef

Louise Pickford
Banh Mi Rice Bowl
BBQ Pork Noodle Bowls with Dipping Sauce
Beef Dolt Bibimbap
Bibimbap Salad with Seared Beef
Burmese-style Spiced Pork with Sweet Garlic Sauce
Crispy 5-Spice Tofu with Sweet & Sour Chilli Sauce
Gochujang-Glazed Mushroom & Wholegrain Rice Bowls
Prawn, Crab & Tamarind Rice Noddles
Spicy Barbecue Korean Beef Rice Bowl

James Porter
Chipotle Crema
Kalua Chipotle Ketchup
Miso Butterfish
Sesame Ginger Fish
Shoyu Chicken
Sticky Aubergine Poke with Sour Carrot Salad
Teriyaki Burger
Teriyaki Sauce

Milli Taylor
Chinese Duck Breast Pancakes with Ginger Jammy Plums

Chef Tee
Jerk Wings with Sticky Rum Sauce

PHOTOGRAPHY CREDITS

Peter Cassidy
Pages 1, 51, 69, 78, 79, 84, 111, 115.

Helen Cathcart
Page 19.

Tara Fisher
Page 61.

Louise Hagger
Pages 22, 23, 24, 29, 98.

Richard Jung
Pages 40, 133.

Mowie Kay
Pages 5, 6, 30, 44, 47, 48, 75, 107, 119, 120, 123, 124, 127, 128, 132, 135, 138.

Erin Kunkel
Page 80.

Steve Painter
Pages 108, 116, 140.

William Reavell
Page 127.

Christopher Scholey
Page 139.

Toby Scott
Pages 55, 56, 57, 59, 60, 63, 64, 67, 68.

Yuki Sugiura
Pages 11, 15, 18, 20, 35, 95.

Ian Wallace
Pages 2, 36, 37, 39, 88, 91, 92, 93, 96, 100, 101, 103, 104.

Kate Whittaker
Pages 33, 42, 43.

Clare Winfield
Pages 12, 13, 32, 71, 72, 76, 83, 99, 130, 137.